Loving praise for

↘ C. S. LEWIS ↙

"We owed each a great debt to the other, and that tie with the deep affection it begot, remains. He was a great man."

J. R. R. Tolkien

"Lewis struck me as the most thoroughly converted man I ever met. Christianity was never for him a separate department of life...His whole vision of life was such that the natural and the supernatural seemed inseparably combined."

Walter Hooper

C.S. LEWIS

THE GRAND MIRACLE

AND OTHER
SELECTED ESSAYS
ON THEOLOGY AND
ETHICS FROM
GOD IN THE DOCK

edited by Walter Hooper

BALLANTINE BOOKS • NEW YORK

Library of Congress Catalog Card Number: 70-129851

ISBN 0-345-30539-6

This edition published by arrangement with William B. Eerdmans Publishing Company

Printed in Canada

First Ballantine Books Edition: April 1983

CONTENTS

1.

MIRACLES

I HAVE KNOWN ONLY ONE PERSON IN MY LIFE WHO claimed to have seen a ghost. It was a woman; and the interesting thing is that she disbelieved in the immortality of the soul before seeing the ghost and still disbelieves after having seen it. She thinks it was a hallucination. In other words, seeing is not believing. This is the first thing to get clear in talking about miracles. Whatever experiences we may have, we shall not regard them as miraculous if we already hold a philosophy which excludes the supernatural. Any event which is claimed as a miracle is, in the last resort, an experience received from the senses; and the senses are not infallible. We can always say we have been the victims of an illusion; if we disbelieve in the supernatural this is what we always shall say. Hence, whether miracles have really ceased or not, they would certainly appear to cease in Western Europe as materialism became the popular creed. For let us make no mistake. If the end of the world appeared in all the literal trappings of the Apocalypse,[1] if the modern materialist saw with his own eyes the heavens rolled up[2] and the great white throne appearing,[3] if he had the sensation of being himself hurled into the Lake of Fire,[4] he would continue forever, in that lake itself, to regard his experience as an illusion and to find the explanation of it in psychoanalysis, or cerebral pathology. Experience by itself proves nothing. If a man doubts whether he is dreaming or waking, no experiment can solve his doubt, since every experiment may itself be part of the dream. Experience proves

[1]The book of Revelation.
[2]*Ibid.*, vi. 14.
[3]*Ibid.*, xx. 11.
[4]*Ibid.*, xix. 20; xx. 10; xx. 14–15; xxi. 8.

this, or that, or nothing, according to the preconceptions we bring to it.

This fact, that the interpretation of experiences depends on preconceptions, is often used as an argument against miracles. It is said that our ancestors, taking the supernatural for granted and greedy of wonders, read the miraculous into events that were really not miracles. And in a sense I grant it. That is to say, I think that just as our preconceptions would prevent us from apprehending miracles if they really occurred, so their preconceptions would lead them to imagine miracles even if they did not occur. In the same way, the doting man will think his wife faithful when she is not and the suspicious man will not think her faithful when she is: the question of her actual fidelity remains, meanwhile, to be settled, if at all, on other grounds. But there is one thing often said about our ancestors we must *not* say. We must not say "They believed in miracles because they did not know the Laws of Nature." This is nonsense. When St. Joseph discovered that his bride was pregnant, he was "minded to put her away."[5] He knew enough biology for that. Otherwise, of course he would not have regarded pregnancy as a proof of infidelity. When he accepted the Christian explanation, he regarded it as a miracle precisely because he knew enough of the Laws of Nature to know that this was a suspension of them. When the disciples saw Christ walking on the water they were frightened:[6] they would not have been frightened unless they had known the Laws of Nature and known that this was an exception. If a man had no conception of a regular order in Nature, then of course he could not notice departures from that order: just as a dunce who does not understand the normal meter of a poem is also unconscious of the poet's variations from it. Nothing is wonderful except the abnormal and nothing is abnormal until we have grasped the norm. Complete ignorance of the Laws of Nature would preclude the perception of the miraculous just as rigidly as complete disbelief in the supernatural precludes it, perhaps even more so. For while the materialist would have at least to explain miracles away, the man wholly ignorant of Nature would simply not notice them.

The experience of a miracle in fact requires two conditions. First we must believe in a normal stability of Nature, which

[5]Matthew i. 19.
[6]Matthew xiv. 26; Mark vi. 49; John vi. 19

means we must recognize that the data offered by our senses recur in regular patterns. Secondly, we must believe in some reality beyond Nature. When both beliefs are held, and not till then, we can approach with an open mind the various reports which claim that this super- or extra-natural reality has sometimes invaded and disturbed the sensuous content of space and time which makes our "natural" world. The belief in such a supernatural reality itself can neither be proved nor disproved by experience. The arguments for its existence are metaphysical, and to me conclusive. They turn on the fact that even to think and act in the natural world we have to assume something beyond it and even assume that we partly belong to that something. In order to think we must claim for our own reasoning a validity which is not credible if our own thought is merely a function of our brain, and our brains a by-product of irrational physical processes. In order to act, above the level of mere impulse, we must claim a similar validity for our judgments of good and evil. In both cases we get the same disquieting result. The concept of Nature itself is one we have reached only tacitly by claiming a sort of *super*-natural status for ourselves.

If we frankly accept this position and then turn to the evidence, we find, of course, that accounts of the supernatural meet us on every side. History is full of them—often in the same documents which we accept wherever they do not report miracles. Respectable missionaries report them not infrequently. The whole Church of Rome claims their continued occurrence. Intimate conversation elicits from almost every acquaintance at least one episode in his life which is what he would call "queer" or "rum." No doubt most stories of miracles are unreliable; but then, as anyone can see by reading the papers, so are most stories of all events. Each story must be taken on its merits: what one must not do is to rule out the supernatural as the one impossible explanation. Thus you may disbelieve in the Mons Angels[7] because you cannot find a sufficient number of sensible people who say they saw them. But if you found a sufficient number, it would, in my view, be unreasonable to explain this by collective hallucination. For

[7]Lewis is referring to the story that angels appeared, protecting British troops in their retreat from Mons, France, on August 26, 1914. A recent summary of the event by Jill Kitson "Did Angels appear to British troops at Mons?" is found in *History Makers*, No. 3 (1969), pp. 132–33.

we know enough of psychology to know that spontaneous un-
animity in hallucination is very improbable, and we do not
know enough of the supernatural to know that a manifestation
of angels is equally improbable. The supernatural theory is the
less improbable of the two. When the Old Testament says that
Sennacherib's invasion was stopped by angels,[8] and Herodotus
says it was stopped by a lot of mice who came and ate up all
the bowstrings of his army,[9] an open-minded man will be on
the side of the angels. Unless you start by begging the question,
there is nothing intrinsically unlikely in the existence of angels
or in the action ascribed to them. But mice just don't do these
things.

A great deal of scepticism now current about the miracles
of our Lord does not, however, come from disbelief of all
reality beyond Nature. It comes from two ideas which are
respectable but I think mistaken. In the first place, modern
people have an almost aesthetic dislike of miracles. Admitting
that God can, they doubt if He would. To violate the laws He
Himself has imposed on His creation seems to them arbitrary,
clumsy, a theatrical device only fit to impress savages—a
solecism against the grammar of the universe. In the second
place, many people confuse the Laws of Nature with the laws
of thought and imagine that their reversal or suspension would
be a contradiction in terms—as if the resurrection of the dead
were the same sort of thing as two and two making five.

I have only recently found the answer to the first objection.
I found it first in George MacDonald and then later in St.
Athanasius. This is what St. Athanasius says in his little book
On the Incarnation: "Our Lord took a body like to ours and
lived as a man in order that those who had refused to recognize
Him in His superintendence and captaincy of the whole universe
might come to recognize from the works He did here below in
the body that what dwelled in this body was the Word of God."
This accords exactly with Christ's own account of His miracles:
"The Son can do nothing of Himself, but what He seeth the
Father do."[10] The doctrine, as I understand it, is something like
this:

There is an activity of God displayed throughout creation,
a wholesale activity let us say which men refuse to recognize.

[8]II Kings xix. 35.
[9]Herodotus, Bk. II, Sect. 141.
[10]John v. 19.

The miracles done by God incarnate, living as a man in Palestine, perform the very same things as this wholesale activity, but at a different speed and on a smaller scale. One of their chief purposes is that men, having seen a thing done by personal power on the small scale, may recognize, when they see the same thing done on the large scale, that the power behind it is also personal—is indeed the very same person who lived among us two thousand years ago. The miracles in fact are a retelling in small letters of the very same story which is written across the whole world in letters too large for some of us to see. Of that larger script part is already visible, part is still unsolved. In other words, some of the miracles do locally what God has already done universally: others do locally what He has not yet done, but will do. In that sense, and from our human point of view, some are reminders and others prophecies.

God creates the vine and teaches it to draw up water by its roots and, with the aid of the sun, to turn that water into a juice which will ferment and take on certain qualities. Thus every year, from Noah's time till ours, God turns water into wine. That, men fail to see. Either like the Pagans they refer the process to some finite spirit, Bacchus or Dionysus: or else, like the moderns, they attribute real and ultimate causality to the chemical and other material phenomena which are all that our senses can discover in it. But when Christ at Cana makes water into wine, the mask is off.[11] The miracle has only half its effect if it only convinces us that Christ is God: it will have its full effect if whenever we see a vineyard or drink a glass of wine we remember that here works He who sat at the wedding party in Cana. Every year God makes a little corn into much corn: the seed is sown and there is an increase, and men, according to the fashion of their age, say "It is Ceres, it is Adonis, it is the Corn King," or else "It is the Laws of Nature." The close-up, the translation, of this annual wonder is the feeding of the five thousand.[12] Bread is not made there of nothing. Bread is not made of stones, as the Devil once suggested to our Lord in vain.[13] A little bread is made into much bread. The Son will do nothing but what He sees the Father do. There is, so to speak, a family *style*. The miracles of healing fall into

[11]John ii. 1–11.

[12]Matthew xiv. 15–21; Mark vi. 34–44; Luke ix. 12–17; John vi. 1–11.

[13]Matthew iv. 3; Luke iv. 3.

the same pattern. This is sometimes obscured for us by the somewhat magical view we tend to take of ordinary medicine. The doctors themselves do not take this view. The magic is not in the medicine but in the patient's body. What the doctor does is to stimulate Nature's functions in the body, or to remove hindrances. In a sense, though we speak for convenience of healing a cut, every cut heals itself; no dressing will make skin grow over a cut on a corpse. That same mysterious energy which we call gravitational when it steers the planets and biochemical when it heals a body is the efficient cause of all recoveries, and if God exists, that energy, directly or indirectly, is His. All who are cured are cured by Him, the healer within. But once He did it visibly, a Man meeting a man. Where He does not work within in this mode, the organism dies. Hence Christ's one miracle of destruction is also in harmony with God's wholesale activity. His bodily hand held out in symbolic wrath blasted a single fig tree;[14] but no tree died that year in Palestine, or any year, or in any land, or even ever will, save because He has done something, or (more likely) ceased to do something, to it.

When He fed the thousands he multiplied fish as well as bread. Look in every bay and almost every river. This swarming, pulsating fecundity shows He is still at work. The ancients had a god called Genius—the god of animal and human fertility, the presiding spirit of gynecology, embryology, or the marriage bed—the "genial bed" as they called it after its god Genius.[15] As the miracles of wine and bread and healing showed who Bacchus really was, who Ceres, who Apollo, and that all were one, so this miraculous multiplication of fish reveals the real Genius. And with that we stand at the threshold of the miracle which for some reason most offends modern ears. I can understand the man who denies the miraculous altogether; but what is one to make of the people who admit some miracles but deny the Virgin Birth? Is it that for all their lip service to the Laws of Nature there is only one Law of Nature that they really believe? Or is it that they see in this miracle a slur upon sexual intercourse which is rapidly becoming the one thing venerated in a world without veneration? No miracle is in fact

[14]Matthew xxi. 19; Mark xi. 13–20.

[15]For further information on this subject see the chapter on "Genius and Genius" in Lewis's *Studies in Medieval and Renaissance, Literature,* ed. Walter Hooper (Cambridge, 1966), pp. 169–74.

more significant. What happens in ordinary generation? What is a father's function in the act of begetting? A microscopic particle of matter from his body fertilizes the female: and with that microscopic particle passes, it may be, the color of his hair and his great-grandfather's hanging lip, and the human form in all its complexity of bones, liver, sinews, heart, and limbs, and prehuman form which the embryo will recapitulate in the womb. Behind every spermatozoon lies the whole history of the universe: locked within it is no small part of the world's future. That is God's normal way of making a man—a process that takes centuries, beginning with the creation of matter itself, and narrowing to one second and one particle at the moment of begetting. And once again men will mistake the sense impressions which this creative act throws off for the act itself or else refer it to some infinite being such as Genius. Once, therefore, God does it directly, instantaneously; without a spermatozoon, without the millenniums of organic history behind the spermatozoon. There was of course another reason. This time He was creating not simply a man, but the man who was to be Himself: the only true Man. The process which leads to the spermatozoon has carried down with it through the centuries much undesirable silt; the life which reaches us by that normal route is tainted. To avoid that taint, to give humanity a fresh start, He once short-circuited the process. There is a vulgar anti-God paper which some anonymous donor sends me every week. In it I recently saw the taunt that we Christians believe in a God who committed adultery with the wife of a Jewish carpenter. The answer to that is that if you describe the action of God in fertilizing Mary as "adultery," then, in that sense, God would have committed adultery with every women who ever had a baby. For what He did once without a human father, He does always even when He uses a human father as His instrument. For the human father in ordinary generation is only a carrier, sometimes an unwilling carrier, always the last in a long line of carriers, of life that comes from the supreme life. Thus the filth that our poor, muddled, sincere, resentful enemies fling at the Holy One, either does not stick, or, sticking, turns into glory.

So much for the miracles which do small and quick what we have already seen in the large letters of God's universal activity. But before I go on to the second class—those which foreshadow parts of the universal activity we have not yet seen—I must guard against a misunderstanding. Do not imagine I am trying to make the miracle less miraculous. I am not arguing that they are more probable because they are less unlike natural events: I am trying to answer those who think them arbitrary, theatrical, unworthy of God, meaningless interruptions of universal order. They remain in my view wholly miraculous. To do instantly with dead and baked corn what ordinarily happens slowly with live seed is just as great a miracle as to make bread of stones. Just as great, but a different *kind* of miracle. That is the point. When I open Ovid,[16] or Grimm,[17] I find the sort of miracles which really would be arbitrary. Trees talk, houses turn into trees, magic rings raise tables richly spread with food in lonely places, ships become goddesses, and men are changed into snakes or birds or bears. It is fun to read about: the least suspicion that it had really happened would turn that fun into nightmare. You find no miracles of that kind in the Gospels. Such things, if they could be, would prove that some alien power was invading Nature; they would not in the least prove that it was the same power which had made Nature and rules her every day. But the true miracles express not simply a god, but God: that which is outside Nature, not as a foreigner, but as her sovereign. They announce not merely that a king has visited our town, but that it is *the* King, *our* King.

The second class of miracles, on this view, foretell what God has not yet done, but will do, universally. He raised one man (the man who was Himself) from the dead because He will one day raise all men from the dead. Perhaps not only men, for there are hints in the New Testament that all creation will eventually be rescued from decay, restored to shape and subserve the splendor of remade humanity.[18] The Transfiguration[19] and the walking on the water[20] are glimpses of the beauty and the effortless power over all matter which will belong to men when they are really waked by God. Now resurrection certainly involves "reversal" of natural process in the sense that it involves a series of changes moving in the

[16]The reference is to Ovid's (43 B.C.–A.D. 18) *Metamorphoses*.

[17]The fairy tales of the brothers, Jacob Ludwig Carl (1785–1863) and Wilhelm Carl (1786–1859) Grimm.

[18]E.g. Romans viii. 22: "We know that the whole creation groaneth and travaileth in pain together until now."

[19]Matthew xvii. 1–9; Mark ix. 2–10.

[20]Matthew xiv. 26; Mark vi. 49; John vi. 19.

opposite direction to those we see. At death, matter which has been organic, falls back gradually into the inorganic, to be finally scattered and used perhaps in other organisms. Resurrection would be the reverse process. It would not of course mean the restoration to each personality of those very atoms, numerically the same, which had made its first or "natural" body. There would not be enough to go round, for one thing; and for another, the unity of the body even in this life was consistent with a slow but perplexed change of its actual ingredients. But it certainly does mean matter of some kind rushing toward organism as now we see it rushing away. It means, in fact, playing backwards a film we have already seen played forwards. In that sense it is a reversal of Nature. But, of course, it is a further question whether reversal in this sense is necessarily contradiction. Do we know that the film cannot be played backwards?

Well, in one sense, it is precisely the teaching of modern physics that the film never works backwards. For modern physics, as you have heard before, the universe is "running down." Disorganization and chance is continually increasing. There will come a time, not infinitely remote, when it will be wholly run down or wholly disorganized, and science knows of no possible return from that state. There must have been a time, not infinitely remote, in the past when it was wound up, though science knows of no winding-up process. The point is that for our ancestors the universe was a picture: for modern physics it is a story. If the universe is a picture these things either appear in that picture or not; and if they don't, since it is an infinite picture, one may suspect that they are contrary to the nature of things. But a story is a different matter; specially if it is an incomplete story. And the story told by modern physics might be told briefly in the words "Humpty Dumpty was falling." That is, it proclaims itself an incomplete story. There must have been a time before he fell, when he was sitting on the wall; there must be a time after he had reached the ground. It is quite true that science knows of no horses and men who can put him together again once he has reached the ground and broken. But then she also knows of no means by which he could originally have been put on the wall. You wouldn't expect her to. All science rests on observation: all our observations are taken *during* Humpty Dumpty's fall, because we were born after he lost his seat on the wall and shall be extinct long before he reaches the ground. But to assume from observations taken while the clock is running down that the unimaginable winding up which must have preceded this process cannot occur when the process is over is the merest dogmatism. From the very nature of the case the laws of degradation and disorganization which we find in matter at present, cannot be the ultimate and eternal nature of things. If they were, there would have been nothing to degrade and disorganize. Humpty Dumpty can't fall off a wall that never existed.

Obviously, an event which lies outside the falling or dis-integrating process which we know as Nature, is not imaginable. If anything is clear from the records of our Lord's appearances after His resurrection, it is that the risen body was very different from the body that died and that it lives under conditions quite unlike those of natural life. It is frequently not recognized by those who see it:[21] and it is not related to space in the same way as our bodies. The sudden appearances and disappearances[22] suggest the ghost of popular tradition: yet He emphatically insists that He is not merely a spirit and takes steps to demonstrate that the risen body can still perform animal operations, such as eating.[23] What makes all this baffling to us is our assumption that to pass beyond what we call Nature— beyond the three dimensions and the five highly specialized and limited senses—is immediately to be in a world of pure negative spirituality, a world where space of any sort and sense of any sort has no function. I know no grounds for believing this. To explain even an atom Schrödinger[24] wants seven dimensions: and give us new senses and we should find a new Nature. There may be Natures piled upon Natures, each supernatural to the one beneath it, before we come to the abyss of pure spirit; and to be in that abyss, at the right hand of the Father, may not mean being absent from any of these Natures— may mean a yet more dynamic presence on all levels. That is why I think it very rash to assume that the story of the Ascension is mere allegory. I know it sounds like the work of people who imagined an absolute up and down and a local heaven in the sky. But to say this is after all to say, "Assuming that the story is fake, we could thus explain how it arose." Without that assumption we find ourselves "moving about in worlds

---

[21]Luke xxiv. 13–31, 36–7; John xx. 14–16.

[22]Mark xvi. 14; Luke xxiv. 31, 36; John xx. 19, 26.

[23]Luke xxiv. 42–3; John xxi. 13.

[24]Arthur Schrödinger (1887–1961), the Austrian physicist.

unrealized"[25] with no probability—or improbability—to guide us. For if the story is true, then a being still in some mode, though not our mode, corporeal, withdrew at His own will from the Nature presented by our three dimensions and five senses, not necessarily into the nonsensuous and undimensioned but possibly into, or through, a world or worlds of supersense and superspace. And He might choose to do it gradually. Who on earth knows what the spectators might see? If they say they saw a momentary movement along the vertical plane—then an indistinct mass—then nothing—who is to pronounce this improbable?

My time is nearly up and I must be very brief with the second class of people whom I promised to deal with: those who mistake the Laws of Nature for laws of thought and, therefore, think that any departure from them is a self-contradiction, like a square circle or two and two making five. To think this is to imagine that the normal processes of Nature are transparent to the intellect, that we can say why she behaves as she does. For, of course, if we cannot see why a thing is so, then we cannot see any reason why it should not be otherwise. But in fact the actual course of Nature is wholly inexplicable. I don't mean that science has not yet explained it, but may do so some day. I mean that the very nature of explanation makes it impossible that we should even explain why matter has the properties it has. For explanation, by its very nature, deals with a world of "ifs and ands." Every explanation takes the form "Since A, therefore B" or "If C, then D." In order to explain any event you have to assume the universe as a going concern, a machine working in a particular way. Since this particular way of working is a basis of all explanation, it can never be itself explained. We can see no reason why it should not have worked in a different way.

To say this is not only to remove the suspicion that miracle is self-contradictory, but also to realize how deeply right St. Athanasius was when he found an essential likeness between the miracles of our Lord and the general order of Nature. Both are a full stop for the explaining intellect. If the "natural" means that which can be fitted into a class, that which obeys a norm, that which can be paralleled, that which can be explained by reference to other events, then Nature herself as a whole is *not*

---

[25]This is probably a misquotation of Wordsworth's "Moving about in worlds not realized." "Intimations of Immortality," ix. 149.

natural. If a miracle means that which must simply be accepted, the unanswerable actuality which gives no account of itself but simply *is*, then the universe is one great miracle. To direct us to that great miracle is one main object of the earthly acts of Christ: that are, as He himself said, Signs.[26] They serve to remind us that the explanations of particular events which we derive *from* the given, the unexplained, the almost willful character of the actual universe, are not explanations of that character. These Signs do not take us away from reality; they recall us to it—recall us from our dreamworld of "ifs and ands" to the stunning actuality of everything that is real. They are focal points at which more reality becomes visible than we ordinarily see at once. I have spoken of how He made miraculous bread and wine and of how, when the Virgin conceived, He had shown Himself the true Genius whom men had ignorantly worshiped long before. It goes deeper than that. Bread and wine were to have an even more sacred significance for Christians and the act of generations was to be the chosen symbol among all mystics for the union of the soul with God. These things are no accidents. With Him there are no accidents. When He created the vegetable world He knew already what dreams the annual death and resurrection of the corn would cause to stir in pious Pagan minds, He knew already that He Himself must so die and live again and in what sense, including and far transcending the old religion of the Corn King. He would say "This is my Body."[27] *Common* bread, miraculous bread, sacramental bread—these three are distinct, but not to be separated. Divine reality is like a fugue. All His acts are different, but they all rhyme or echo to one another. It is this that makes Christianity so difficult to talk about. Fix your mind on any one story or any one doctrine and it becomes at once a magnet to which truth and glory come rushing from all levels of being. Our featureless pantheistic unities and glib rationalist distinctions are alike defeated by the seamless, yet ever-varying texture of reality, the liveness, the elusiveness, the intertwined harmonies of the multidimensional fertility of God. But if this is the difficulty, it is also one of the firm grounds of our belief. To think that this was a fable, a product of our own brains as they are a product of matter, would be to believe that this vast

[26]Matthew xii. 39; xvi. 4; xxiv. 24, 30; Mark xiii. 22; xvi. 17, 20; Luke xxi. 11, 25.

[27]Matthew xxvi. 26; Mark xiv. 22; Luke xxii, 19; I Corinthians xi. 24.

symphonic splendor had come out of something much smaller and emptier than itself. It is not so. We are nearer to the truth in the vision seen by Julian of Norwich, when Christ appeared to her holding in His hand a little thing like a hazelnut and saying. "This is all that is created."[28] And it seemed to her so small and weak that she wondered how it could hold together at all.[29]

[28]*Sixteen Revelations of Divine Love*, ed. Roger Hudleston (London, 1927), ch. 5, p. 9.
[29]See Letter 3.

2.

DOGMA AND
THE UNIVERSE

It is a common reproach against Christianity that its dogmas are unchanging, while human knowledge is in continual growth. Hence, to unbelievers, we seem to be always engaged in the hopeless task of trying to force the new knowledge into molds which it has outgrown. I think this feeling alienates the outsider much more than any particular discrepancies between this or that doctrine and this or that scientific theory. We may, as we say, "get over" dozens of isolated "difficulties," but that does not alter his sense that the endeavor as a whole is doomed to failure and perverse: indeed, the more ingenious, the more perverse. For it seems to him clear that, if our ancestors had known what we know about the universe, Christianity would never have existed at all: and, however we patch and mend, no system of thought which claims to be immutable can, in the long run, adjust itself to our growing knowledge.

That is the position I am going to try to answer. But before I go on to what I regard as the fundamental answer, I would like to clear up certain points about the actual relations between Christian doctrine and the scientific knowledge we already have. That is a different matter from the continual growth of knowledge we imagine, whether rightly or wrongly, in the future and which, as some think, is bound to defeat us in the end.

In one respect, as many Christians have noticed, contemporary science has recently come into line with Christian doctrine, and parted company with the classical forms of materialism. If anything emerges clearly from modern physics, it is that nature is not everlasting. The universe had a beginning, and will have an end. But the great materialistic systems of the past all believed in the eternity, and thence in the self-existence of matter. As Professor Whittaker said in the Riddell Lectures of 1942, "It was never possible to oppose seriously the dogma of the Creation except by maintaining that the world has existed from all eternity in more or less its present state."[1] This fundamental ground for materialism has now been withdrawn. We should not lean too heavily on this, for scientific theories change. But at the moment it appears that the burden of proof rests, not on us, but on those who deny that Nature has some cause beyond herself.

In popular thought, however, the origin of the universe has counted (I think) for less than its character—its immense size and its apparent indifference, if not hostility, to human life. And very often this impresses people all the more because it is supposed to be a modern discovery—an excellent example of those things which our ancestors did not know and which, if they had known them, would have prevented the very beginnings of Christianity. Here there is a simple historical falsehood. Ptolemy knew just as well as Eddington[2] that the earth was infinitesimal in comparison with the whole content of space.[3] There is no question here of knowledge having grown until the frame of archaic thought is no longer able to contain it. The real question is why the spatial insignificance of the earth, after being known for centuries, should suddenly in the last century have become an argument against Christianity. I do not know why this has happened; but I am sure it does not mark an increased clarity of thought, for the argument from size is, in my opinion, very feeble.

When the doctor at a postmortem diagnoses poison, pointing to the state of the dead man's organs, his argument is rational because he has a clear idea of that opposite state in which the organs would have been found if no poison were present. In the same way, if we use the vastness of space and the smallness of earth to disprove the existence of God, we ought to have a clear idea of the sort of universe we should expect if God did exist. But have we? Whatever space may be in itself—and, of course, some moderns think it finite—we certainly perceive it as three-dimensional, and to three-dimensional space we can conceive no boundaries. By the very forms of our perceptions,

[1] Sir Edmund Taylor Whittaker, *The Beginning and End of the World*, Riddell Memorial Lectures, Fourteenth Series (Oxford, 1942), p. 40.

[2] Sir Arthur Stanley Eddington (1882–1944) who wrote *The Expanding Universe* (1933).

[3] Ptolemy lived at Alexandria in the second century A.D. The reference is to his *Almagest*, bk. I, ch. v.

therefore, we must feel as if we lived somewhere in infinite space. If we discovered no objects in this infinite space except those which are of use to man (our own sun and moon), then this vast emptiness would certainly be used as a strong argument against the existence of God. If we discover other bodies, they must be habitable or uninhabitable: and the odd thing is that both these hypotheses are used as grounds for rejecting Christianity. If the universe is teeming with life, this, we are told, reduces to absurdity the Christian claim—or what is thought to be the Christian claim—that man is unique, and the Christian doctrine that to this one planet God came down and was incarnate for us men and our salvation. If, on the other hand, the earth is really unique, then that proves that life is only an accidental by-product in the universe, and so again disproves our religion. Really, we are hard to please. We treat God as the police treat a man when he is arrested; whatever He does will be used in evidence against Him. I do not think this is due to our wickedness. I suspect there is something in our very mode of thought which makes it inevitable that we should always be baffled by actual existence, *whatever* character actual existence may have. Perhaps a finite and contingent creature—a creature that might not have existed—will always find it hard to acquiesce in the brute fact that it is, here and now, attached to an actual order of things.

However that may be, it is certain that the whole argument from size rests on the assumption that differences of size ought to coincide with differences of value: for unless they do, there is, of course, no reason why the minute earth and the yet smaller human creatures upon it should not be the most important things in a universe that contains the spiral nebulae. Now, is this assumption rational or emotional? I feel, as well as anyone else, the absurdity of supposing that the galaxy could be of less moment in God's eyes than such an atom as a human being. But I notice that I feel no similar absurdity in supposing that a man of five feet high may be more important than another man who is five feet three and a half—nor that a man may matter more than a tree, or a brain more than a leg. In other words, the feeling of absurdity arises only if the differences of size are very great. But where a relation is perceived by reason it holds good universally. If size and value had any real connection, small differences in size would accompany small differences in value as surely as large differences in size accompany large differences in value. But no sane man could suppose that this is so. I don't think the taller man *slightly* more valuable than the shorter one. I don't allow a slight superiority to trees over men, and then neglect it because it is too small to bother about. I perceive as long as I am dealing with the small differences of size, that they have no connection with value whatsoever. I therefore conclude that the importance attached to the great differences of size is an affair, not of reason but of emotion—of that peculiar emotion which superiorities in size produce only after a certain point of absolute size has been reached.

We are inveterate poets. Our imaginations awake. Instead of mere quantity, we now have a quality—the sublime. Unless this were so, the merely arithmetical greatness of the galaxy would be no more impressive than the figures in a telephone directory. It is thus, in a sense, from ourselves that the material universe derives its power to overawe us. To a mind which did not share our emotions, and lacked our imaginative energies, the argument from size would be sheerly meaningless. Men look on the starry heavens with reverence: monkeys do not. The silence of the eternal spaces terrified Pascal,[4] but it was the greatness of Pascal that enabled them to do so. When we are frightened by the greatness of the universe, we are (almost literally) frightened by our own shadows: for these light years and billions of centuries are mere arithmetic until the shadow of man, the poet, the maker of myth, falls upon them. I do not say we are wrong to tremble at his shadow; it is a shadow of an image of God. But if ever the vastness of matter threatens to overcross our spirits, one must remember that it is matter spiritualized which does so. To puny man, the great nebula in Andromeda owes in a sense its greatness.

And this drives me to say yet again that we are hard to please. If the world in which we found ourselves were not vast and strange enough to give us Pascal's terror, what poor creatures we should be! Being what we are, rational but also animate, amphibians who start from the world of sense and proceed through myth and metaphor to the world of spirit, I do not see how we could have come to know the greatness of God without that hint furnished by the greatness of the material universe. Once again, what sort of universe do we demand? If it were small enough to be cozy, it would not be big enough to be sublime. If it is large enough for us to stretch our spiritual limbs in, it must be large enough to baffle us. Cramped or

[4]Blaise Pascal, *Pensées*, No. 206.

terrified, we must, in any conceivable world, be one or the other. I prefer terror. I should be suffocated in a universe that I could see to the end of. Have you never, when walking in a wood, turned back deliberately for fear you should come out at the other side and thus make it ever after in your imagination a mere beggarly strip of trees?

I hope you do not think I am suggesting that God made the spiral nebulae solely or chiefly in order to give me the experience of awe and bewilderment. I have not the faintest idea why He made them; on the whole, I think it would be rather surprising if I had. As far as I understand the matter, Christianity is not wedded to an anthropocentric view of the universe as a whole. The first chapters of Genesis, no doubt, give the story of creation in the form of a folktale—a fact recognized as early as the time of St. Jerome—and if you take them alone you might get that impression. But it is not confirmed by the Bible as a whole. There are few places in literature where we are more sternly warned against making man the measure of all things than in the Book of Job: "Canst thou draw out leviathan with an hook? Will he make a covenant with thee? Wilt thou take him for a servant? Shall not one be cast down even at the sight of him?"[5] In St. Paul, the power of the skies seem usually to be hostile to man. It is, of course, the essence of Christianity that God loves man and for his sake became man and died. But that does not prove that man is the sole end of nature. In the parable, it was the one lost sheep that the shepherd went in search of:[6] it was not the only sheep in the flock, and we are not told that it was the most valuable—save insofar as the most desperately in need has, while the needs lasts, a peculiar value in the eyes of Love. The doctrine of the Incarnation would conflict with what we know of this vast universe only if we knew also that there were other rational species in it who had, like us, fallen, and who needed redemption in the same mode, and that they had not been vouchsafed it. But we know none of these things. It may be full of life that needs no redemption. It may be full of life that has been redeemed. It may be full of things quite other than life which satisfy the Divine Wisdom in fashions one cannot conceive. We are in no position to draw up maps of God's psychology, and prescribe limits to His interests. We would not do so even for a man

[5]Job xli. 1, 4, 9.
[6]Matthew xviii. 12; Luke xv. 4.

whom we knew to be greater than ourselves. The doctrines that God is love and that He delights in men, are positive doctrines, not limiting doctrines. He is not less than this. What more He may be, we do not know; we know only that He must be more than we can conceive. It is to be expected that His creation should be, in the main, unintelligible to us.

Christians themselves have been much to blame for the misunderstanding on these matters. They have a bad habit of talking as if revelation existed to gratify curiosity by illuminating all creation so that it becomes self-explanatory and all questions are answered. But revelation appears to me to be purely practical, to be addressed to the particular animal, Fallen Man, for the relief of his urgent necessities—not to the spirit of inquiry in man for the gratification of his liberal curiosity. We know that God has visited and redeemed His people, and that tells us just as much about the general character of the creation as a dose given to one sick hen on a big farm tells it about the general character of farming in England. What we must do, which road we must take to the fountain of life, we know, and none who has seriously followed the directions complains that he has been deceived. But whether there are other creatures like ourselves, and how they are dealt with: whether inanimate matter exists only to serve living creatures or for some other reason: whether the immensity of space is a means to some end, or an illusion, or simply the natural mode in which infinite energy might be expected to create—on all these points I think we are left to our own speculations.

No. It is not Christianity which need fear the giant universe. It is those systems which place the whole meaning of existence in biological or social evolution on our own planet. It is the creative evolutionist, the Bergsonian or Shavian, or the Communist, who should tremble when he looks up at the night sky. For he really is committed to a sinking ship. He really is attempting to ignore the discovered nature of things, as though by concentrating on the possibly upward trend in a single planet he could make himself forget the inevitable downward trend in the universe as a whole, the trend to low temperatures and irrevocable disorganization. For entropy is the real cosmic wave, and evolution only a momentary tellurian ripple within it.

On these grounds, then, I submit that we Christians have as little to fear as anyone from the knowledge actually acquired. But, as I said at the beginning, that is not the fundamental answer. The endless fluctuations of scientific theory which seem today so much friendlier to us than in the last century may turn against us tomorrow. The basic answer lies elsewhere.

Let me remind you of the question we are trying to answer. It is this: How can an unchanging system survive the continual increase of knowledge? Now, in certain cases we know very well how it can. A mature scholar reading a great passage in Plato, and taking in at one glance the metaphysics, the literary beauty, and the place of both in the history of Europe, is in a very different position from a boy learning the Greek alphabet. Yet through that unchanging system of the alphabet all this vast mental and emotional activity is operating. It has not been broken by the new knowledge. It is not outworn. If it changed, all would be chaos. A great Christian statesman, considering the morality of a measure which will affect millions of lives, and which involves economic, geographical, and political considerations of the utmost complexity, is in a different position from a boy first learning that one must not cheat or tell lies, or hurt innocent people. But only insofar as that first knowledge of the great moral platitudes survives unimpaired in the statesman will his deliberation be moral at all. If that goes, then there has been no progress, but only mere change. For change is not progress unless the core remains unchanged. A small oak grows into a big oak: if it became a beech, that would not be growth, but mere change. And thirdly, there is a great difference between counting apples and arriving at the mathematical formulae of modern physics. But the multiplication table is used in both and does not grow out of date.

In other words, wherever there is real progress in knowledge, there is some knowledge that is not superseded. Indeed, the very possibility of progress demands that there should be an unchanging element. New bottles for new wine, by all means: but not new palates, throats, and stomachs, or it would not be, for us, "wine" at all. I take it we should all agree to find this sort of unchanging element in the simple rules of mathematics. I would add to these the primary principles of morality. And I would also add the fundamental doctrines of Christianity. To put it in rather more technical language, I claim that the positive historical statements made by Christianity have the power, elsewhere found chiefly in formal principles, of receiving, without intrinsic change, the increasing complexity of meaning which increasing knowledge puts into them.

For example, it may be true (though I don't for a moment suppose it is) that when the Nicene Creed said "He came down from Heaven," the writers had in mind a local movement from a local heaven to the surface of the earth—like a parachute descent. Others since may have dismissed the idea of a spatial heaven altogether. But neither the significance nor the credibility of what is asserted seems to be in the least affected by the change. On either view, the thing is miraculous: on either view, the mental images which attend the act of belief are inessential. When a Central African convert and a Harley Street specialist both affirm that Christ rose from the dead, there is, no doubt, a very great difference between their thoughts. To one, the simple picture of a dead body getting up is sufficient: the other may think of a whole series of biochemical and even physical processes beginning to work backwards. The doctor knows that, in his experience, they never have worked backwards; but the Negro knows that dead bodies don't get up and walk. Both are faced with miracle, and both know it. If both think miracle impossible, the only difference is that the doctor will expound the impossibility in much greater detail, will give an elaborate gloss on the simple statement that dead men don't walk about. If both believe, all the doctor says will merely analyze and explicate the words "He rose." When the author of Genesis says that God made man in His own image, he may have pictured a vaguely corporeal God making man as a child makes a figure out of plasticine. A modern Christian philosopher may think of a process lasting from the first creation of matter to the final appearance on this planet of an organism fit to receive spiritual as well as biological life. But both mean essentially the same thing. Both are denying the same thing— the doctrine that matter by some blind power inherent in itself has produced spirituality.

Does this mean that Christians on different levels of general education conceal radically different beliefs under an identical form of words? Certainly not. For what they agree on is the substance, and what they differ about is the shadow. When one imagines his God seated in a local heaven above a flat earth, where another sees God and creation in terms of Professor Whitehead's philosophy,[7] this difference touches precisely what does not matter. Perhaps this seems to you an exaggeration. But is it? As regards material reality, we are now being forced to the conclusion that we know nothing about it

---

[7]Alfred North Whitehead (1867–1947), who wrote, among other works, *Science and the Modern World* (1925) and *Religion in the Making* (1926).

save its mathematics. The tangible beach and pebbles of our first calculators, the imaginable atoms of Democritus, the plain man's picture of space, turn out to be the shadow: numbers are the substance of our knowledge, the sole liaison between mind and things. What nature is in herself evades us; what seem to naive perception to be the evident things about her, turn out to be the most phantasmal. It is something the same with our knowledge of spiritual reality. What God is in Himself, how He is to be conceived by philosophers, retreats continually from our knowledge. The elaborate world pictures which accompany religion and which look each so solid while they last, turn out to be only shadows. It is religion itself—prayer and sacrament and repentance and adoration—which is here, in the long run, our sole avenue to the real. Like mathematics, religion can grow from within, or decay. The Jew knows more than the Pagan, the Christian more than the Jew, the modern vaguely religious man less than any of the three. But, like mathematics, it remains simply itself, capable of being applied to any new theory of the material universe and outmoded by none.

When any man comes into the presence of God he will find, whether he wishes it or not, that all those things which seemed to make him so different from the men of other times, or even from his earlier self, have fallen off him. He is back where he always was, where every man always is. *Eadem sunt omnia semper*.[8] Do not let us deceive ourselves. No possible complexity which we can give to our picture of the universe can hide us from God: there is no copse, no forest, no jungle thick enough to provide cover. We read in Revelation of Him that sat on the throne "from whose face the earth and heaven fled away."[9] It may happen to any of us at any moment. In the twinkling of an eye, in a time too small to be measured, and in any place, all that seems to divide us from God can flee away, vanish, leaving us naked before Him, like the first man, like the only man, as if nothing but He and I existed. And since that contact cannot be avoided for long, and since it means either bliss or horror, the business of life is to learn to like it. That is the first and great commandment.

[8]"Everything is always the same."
[9]Revelation xx. 11.

3.

ANSWERS TO QUESTIONS ON CHRISTIANITY

[The answers to questions printed here were given by
Lewis at a "One Man Brains Trust" held on April 18,
1944, at the Head Office of Electric and Musical Indus-
tries Ltd., Hayes, Middlesex. Shorthand notes were made
and a typescript was sent to Lewis. He revised it a little,
and it was printed in 1944. Mr. H. W. Bowen was the
question master.]

Lewis:
I have been asked to open with a few words on Christianity
and modern industry. Now modern industry is a subject of
which I know nothing at all. But for that very reason it may
illustrate what Christianity, in my opinion, does and does not
do. Christianity does *not* replace the technical. When it tells
you to feed the hungry it doesn't give you lessons in cookery.
If you want to learn *that,* you must go to a cook rather than a
Christian. If you are not a professional economist and have no
experience of industry, simply being a Christian won't give
you the answer to industrial problems. My own idea is that
modern industry is a radically hopeless system. You can improve wages, hours, conditions, etc., but all that doesn't cure
the deepest trouble: i.e., that numbers of people are kept all
their lives doing dull repetition work which gives no full play
to their faculties. How that is to be overcome, I do not know.
If a single country abandoned the system it would merely fall
a prey to the other countries which hadn't abandoned it. I don't
know the solution: that is not the kind of thing Christianity
teaches a person like me. Let's now carry on with the questions.

Question 1.
    Christians are taught to love their neighbors. How, there-
fore, can they justify their attitude of supporting the war?

Lewis:

You are told to love your neighbors as yourself. How do you love yourself? When I look into my own mind, I find that I do not love myself by thinking myself a dear old chap or having affectionate feelings. I do not think that I love myself because I am particularly good, but just because I am myself and quite apart from my character. I might detest something which I have done. Nevertheless, I do not cease to love myself. In other words, that definite distinction that Christians make between hating sin and loving the sinner is one that you have been making in your own case since you were born. You dislike what you have done, but you don't cease to love yourself. You may even think that you ought to be hanged. You may even think that you ought to go to the police and own up and be hanged. Love is not affectionate feeling, but a steady wish for the loved person's ultimate good as far as it can be obtained. It seems to me, therefore, that when the worst comes to the worst, if you cannot restrain a man by any method except by trying to kill him, then a Christian must do that. That is my answer. But I may be wrong. It is very difficult to answer, of course.

Question 2.

Supposing a factory worker asked you: "How can I find God?" How would you reply?

Lewis:

I don't see how the problem would be different for a factory worker than for anyone else. The primary thing about any man is that he is a human being, sharing all the ordinary human temptations and assets. What is the special problem about the factory worker? But perhaps it is worth saying this:

Christianity really does two things about conditions here and now in this world:

(1) It tries to make them as good as possible, i.e., to reform them; but also

(2) It fortifies you against them insofar as they remain bad.

If what was in the questioner's mind was this problem of repetition work, then the factory worker's difficulty is the same as any other man confronted with any sorrow or difficulty. People will find God if they consciously seek from Him the right attitude toward all unpleasant things . . . if that is the point of the question?

Question 3.

Will you please say how you would define a practicing Christian? Are there any other varieties?

Lewis:

Certainly there are a great many other varieties. It depends, of course, on what you mean by "practicing Christian." If you mean one who has practiced Christianity in every respect at every moment of his life, then there is only one on record— Christ Himself. In that sense there are no practicing Christians, but only Christians who, in varying degrees, try to practice it and fail in varying degrees and then start again. A perfect practice of Christianity would, of course, consist in a perfect imitation of the life of Christ—I mean, insofar as it was applicable in one's own particular circumstances. Not in an idiotic sense—it doesn't mean that every Christian should grow a beard, or be a bachelor, or become a traveling preacher. It means that every single act and feeling, every experience, whether pleasant or unpleasant, must be referred to God. It means looking at everything as something that comes from Him, and always looking to Him and asking His will first, and saying: "How would He wish me to deal with this?"

A kind of picture or pattern (in a very remote way) of the relation between the perfect Christian and his God, would be the relation of the good dog to its master. This is only a very imperfect picture, though, because the dog hasn't reason like its master: whereas we do share in God's reason, even if in an imperfect and interrupted way ("interrupted" because we don't think rationally for very long at a time—it's too tiring—and we haven't information to understand things fully, and our intelligence itself has certain limitations). In that way we are more like God than the dog is like us, though, of course, there are other ways in which the dog is more like us than we are like God. It is only an illustration.

Question 4.

What justification on ethical grounds and on the grounds of social expediency exists for the church's attitude toward venereal disease and prophylaxis and publicity in connection with it?

Lewis:

I need further advice on that question, and then perhaps I can answer it. Can the questioner say which church he has in mind?

Voice.

The church concerned is the Church of England, and its attitude, though not written, is implicit in that it has more or less banned all publicity in connection with prophylactic methods of combating venereal disease. The view of some is that moral punishment should not be avoided.

Lewis:

I haven't myself met any clergymen of the church of England who held that view: and I don't hold it myself. There are obvious objections to it. After all, it isn't only venereal disease that can be regarded as a punishment for bad conduct. Indigestion in old age may be the result of overeating in earlier life: but no one objects to advertisements for Beecham's Pills. I, at any rate, strongly dissent from the view you've mentioned.

Question 5.

Many people feel resentful or unhappy because they think they are the target of unjust fate. These feelings are stimulated by bereavement, illness, deranged domestic or working conditions, or the observation of suffering in others. What is the Christian view of this problem?

Lewis:

The Christian view is that men were created to be in a certain relationship to God (if we are in that relation to Him, the right relation to one another will follow inevitably). Christ said it was difficult for "the rich" to enter the Kingdom of Heaven,[1] referring, no doubt, to "riches" in the ordinary sense. But I think it really covers riches in every sense—good fortune, health, popularity, and all the things one wants to have. All these things tend—just as money tends—to make you feel independent of God, because if you have them you are happy already and contented in this life. You don't want to turn away to anything more, and so you try to rest in a shadowy happiness as if it could last forever. But God wants to give you a real

[1]Matthew xix. 23; Mark x. 23; Luke xviii. 24.

and eternal happiness. Consequently He may have to take all these "riches" away from you: if He doesn't, you will go on relying on them. It sounds cruel, doesn't it? But I am beginning to find out that what people call the cruel doctrines are really the kindest ones in the long run. I used to think it was a "cruel" doctrine to say that troubles and sorrows were "punishments." But I find in practice that when you are in trouble, the moment you regard it as a "punishment," it becomes easier to bear. If you think of this world as a place intended simply for our happiness, you find it quite intolerable: think of it as a place of training and correction and it's not so bad.

Imagine a set of people all living in the same building. Half of them think it is a hotel, the other half think it is a prison. Those who think it a hotel might regard it as quite intolerable, and those who thought it was a prison might decide that it was really surprisingly comfortable. So that what seems the ugly doctrine is one that comforts and strengthens you in the end. The people who try to hold an optimistic view of this world would become pessimists: the people who hold a pretty stern view of it become optimistic.

Question 6.

Materialists and some astronomers suggest that the solar planetary system and life as we know it was brought about by an accidental stellar collision. What is the Christian view of this theory?

Lewis:

If the solar system was brought about by an accidental collision, then the appearance of organic life on this planet was also an accident, and the whole evolution of man was an accident too. If so, then all our present thoughts are mere accidents—the accidental by-product of the movement of atoms. And this holds for the thoughts of the materialists and astronomers as well as for anyone else's. But if *their* thoughts—i.e., of materialism and astronomy—are merely accidental by-products, why should we believe them to be true? I see no reason for believing that one accident should be able to give me a correct account of all the other accidents. It's like expecting that the accidental shape taken by the splash when you upset a milk jug should give you a correct account of how the jug was made and why it was upset.

Question 7.

Is it true that Christianity (especially the Protestant forms) tends to produce a gloomy, joyless condition of society which is like a pain in the neck to most people?

Lewis:

As to the distinction between Protestant and other forms of Christianity, it is very difficult to answer. I find by reading about the sixteenth century, that people like Sir Thomas More, for whom I have a great respect, always regarded Martin Luther's doctrines not as gloomy thinking, but as wishful thinking. I doubt whether we can make a distinction between Protestant and other forms in this respect. Whether Protestantism is gloomy and whether Christianity at all produces gloominess, I find it very difficult to answer, as I have never lived in a completely non-Christian society nor a completely Christian one, and I wasn't there in the sixteenth century, and only have my knowledge from reading books. I think there is about the same amount of fun and gloom in all periods. The poems, novels, letters, etc., of every period all seem to show that. But again, I don't really know the answer, of course. I wasn't there.

Question 8.

Is it true that Christians must be prepared to live a life of personal discomfort and self-sacrifice in order to qualify for "Pie in the Sky"?

Lewis:

All people, whether Christian or not, must be prepared to live a life of discomfort. It is impossible to accept Christianity for the sake of finding comfort: but the Christian tries to lay himself open to the will of God, to do what God wants him to do. You don't know in advance whether God is going to set you to do something difficult or painful, or something that you will quite like; and some people of heroic mold are disappointed when the job doled out to them turns out to be something quite nice. But you must be prepared for the unpleasant things and the discomforts. I don't mean fasting, and things like that. They are a different matter. When you are training soldiers in maneuvers, you practice in blank ammunition because you would like them to have practice before meeting the real enemy. So we must practice in abstaining from pleasures which are not in themselves wicked. If you don't abstain from pleasure, you won't be good when the time comes along. It is purely a matter of practice.

Voice.

Are not practices like fasting and self-denial borrowed from earlier or more primitive religions?

Lewis:

I can't say for certain which bits came into Christianity from earlier religions. An enormous amount did. I should find it hard to believe Christianity if that were not so. I couldn't believe that nine hundred and ninety-nine religions were completely false and the remaining one true. In reality, Christianity is primarily the fulfillment of the Jewish religion, but also the fulfillment of what was vaguely hinted in all the religions at their best. What was vaguely seen in them all comes into focus in Christianity—just as God Himself comes into focus by becoming a man. I take it that the speaker's remarks on earlier religions are based on evidence about modern savages. I don't think it is good evidence. Modern savages usually represent some decay in culture—you find them doing things which look as if they had a fairly civilized basis once, which they have forgotten. To assume that primitive man was exactly like the modern savage is unsound.

Voice.

Could you say any more on how one discovers whether a task is laid on one by God, or whether it comes in some other way? If we cannot distinguish between the pleasant and the unpleasant things, it is a complicated matter.

Lewis:

We are guided by the ordinary rules of moral behavior, which I think are more or less common to the human race and quite reasonable and demanded by the circumstances. I don't mean anything like sitting down and waiting for a supernatural vision.

Voice.

We don't qualify for heaven by practice, but salvation is obtained at the Cross. We do nothing to obtain it, but follow Christ. We may have pain or tribulation, but nothing we do qualifies us for heaven, but Christ.

Lewis:

The controversy about faith and works is one that has gone on for a very long time, and it is a highly technical matter. I personally rely on the paradoxical text: "Work out your own salvation . . . for it is God that worketh in you."[2] It looks as if in one sense we do nothing, and in another case we do a damned lot. "Work out your own salvation with fear and trembling,"[3] but you must have it in you before you can work it out. But I have no wish to go further into it, as it would interest no one but the Christians present, would it?

Question 9.

Would the application of Christian standards bring to an end or greatly reduce scientific and material progress? In other words, is it wrong for a Christian to be ambitious and strive for personal success?

Lewis:

It is easiest to think of a simplified example. How would the application of Christianity affect anyone on a desert island? Would he be less likely to build a comfortable hut? The answer is "No." There might come a particular moment, of course, when Christianity would tell him to bother less about the hut, i.e., if he were in danger of coming to think that the hut was the most important thing in the universe. But there is no evidence that Christianity would prevent him from building it.

Ambition! We must be careful what we mean by it. If it means the desire to get ahead of other people—which is what I think it does mean—then it is bad. If it means simply wanting to do a thing well, then it is good. It isn't wrong for an actor to want to act his part as well as it can possibly be acted, but the wish to have his name in bigger type than the other actors is a bad one.

Voice.

It's all right to be a general, but if it is one's ambition to be a general, then you shouldn't become one.

Lewis:

The mere event of becoming a general isn't either right or

[2] Philippians ii. 12.
[3] *Ibid.*

wrong in itself. What matters morally is your attitude toward it. The man may be thinking about winning a war; he may be wanting to be a general because he honestly thinks he has a good plan and is glad of a chance to carry it out. That's all right. But if he is thinking: "What can I get out of the job?" or "How can I get on the front page of the *Illustrated News*?" then it is all wrong. And what we call "ambition" usually means the wish to be more conspicuous or more successful than someone else. It is this competitive element in it that is bad. It is perfectly reasonable to want to dance well or to look nice. But when the dominant wish is to dance better or look nicer than the others—when you begin to feel that if the others danced as well as you or looked as nice as you, that would take all the fun out of it—then you are going wrong.

Voice.

I am wondering how far we can ascribe to the work of the Devil those very legitimate desires that we indulge in. Some people have a very sensitive conception of the presence of the Devil. Others haven't. Is the Devil as real as we think he is? That doesn't trouble some people, since they have no desire to be good, but others are continually harassed by the Old Man himself.

Lewis:

No reference to the Devil or devils is included in any Christian Creeds, and it is quite possible to be a Christian without believing in them. I do believe such beings exist, but that is my own affair. Supposing there to be such beings, the degree to which humans were conscious of their presence would presumably vary very much. I mean, the more a man was in the Devil's power, the less he would be aware of it, on the principle that a man is still fairly sober as long as he knows he's drunk. It is the people who are fully awake and trying hard to be good who would be most aware of the Devil. It is when you start arming against Hitler that you first realize your country is full of Nazi agents. Of course, they don't want you to believe in the Devil. If devils exist, their first aim is to give you an anesthetic—to put you off your guard. Only if that fails, do you become aware of them.

Voice.

Does Christianity retard scientific advancement? Or does it

approve of those who help spiritually others who are on the road to perdition, by scientifically removing the environmental causes of the trouble?

Lewis:

Yes. In the abstract it is certainly so. At a particular moment, if most human beings are concentrating only on material improvements in the environment, it may be the duty of Christians to point out (and pretty loudly) that this isn't the only thing that matters. But as a general rule it is in favor of all knowledge and all that will help the human race in any way.

Question 10.

The Bible was written thousands of years ago for people in a lower state of mental development than today. Many portions seems preposterous in the light of modern knowledge. In view of this, should not the Bible be rewritten with the object of discarding the fabulous and reinterpreting the remainder?

Lewis:

First of all as to the people in a lower state of mental development. I am not so sure what lurks behind that. If it means that people ten thousand years ago didn't know a good many things that we know now, of course, I agree. But if it means that there has been any advance in *intelligence* in that time, I believe there is no evidence for any such thing. The Bible can be divided into two parts—the Old and the New Testaments. The Old Testament contains fabulous elements. The New Testament consists mostly of teaching, not of narrative at all: but where it *is* narrative, it is, in my opinion, historical. As to the fabulous element in the Old Testament, I very much doubt if you would be wise to chuck it out. What you get is something *coming gradually into focus*. First you get, scattered through the heathen religions all over the world— but still quite vague and mythical—the idea of a god who is killed and broken and then comes to life again. No one knows where he is supposed to have lived and died; he's not historical. Then you get the Old Testament. Religious ideas get a bit more focused. Everything is now connected with a particular nation. And it comes still more into focus as it goes on. Jonah and the Whale,[4] Noah and his Ark,[5] are fabulous; but the court history

---

[4]The Book of Jonah.

[5]Genesis, chapters vi–viii.

of King David[6] is probably as reliable as the court history of Louis XIV. Then, in the New Testament the *thing really happens*. The dying god really appears—as an historical person, living in a definite place and time. It we *could* sort out all the fabulous elements in the earlier stages and separate them from the historical ones, I think we might lose an essential part of the whole process. That is my own idea.

Question 11.

Which of the religions of the world gives to its followers the greatest happiness?

Lewis:

Which of the religions of the world gives to its followers the greatest happiness? While it lasts, the religion of worshiping oneself is the best.

I have an elderly acquaintance of about eighty, who has lived a life of unbroken selfishness and self-admiration from the earliest years, and is, more or less, I regret to say, one of the happiest men I know. From the moral point of view it is very difficult! I am not approaching the question from that angle. As you perhaps know, I haven't always been a Christian. I didn't go to religion to make me happy. I always knew a bottle of port would do that. If you want a religion to make you feel really comfortable, I certainly don't recommend Christianity. I am certain there must be a patent American article on the market which will suit you far better, but I can't give any advice on it.

Question 12.

Are there any unmistakable outward signs in a person surrendered to God? Would he be cantankerous? Would he smoke?

Lewis:

I think of the advertisements for "White Smiles" toothpaste, saying that it is the best on the market. If they are true, it would follow that:

(1) Anyone who starts using it will have better teeth;

(2) Anyone using it has better teeth than he would have if he weren't using it.

But you can't test it in the case of one who has naturally

[6]II Samuel, ch. ii–I Kings, ch. ii.

bad teeth and uses it, and compare him with a healthy Negro who has never used toothpaste at all.

Take the case of a sour old maid, who is a Christian, but cantankerous. On the other hand, take some pleasant and popular fellow, but who has never been to church. Who knows how much more cantankerous the old maid might be if she were *not* a Christian, and how much more likable the nice fellow might be if he *were* a Christian? You can't judge Christianity simply by comparing the *product* in those two people; you would need to know what kind of raw material Christ was working on in both cases.

As an illustration, let us take a case of industrialism. Let us take two factories:

    Factory A with poor and inadequate plant, and
    Factory B with first-class modern plant

You can't judge by the outside. You must consider the plant and methods by which they are run, and considering the plant at Factory A, it may be a wonder it does anything at all; and considering the new machinery at Factory B, it may be a wonder it doesn't do better.

Question 13.

What is your opinion about raffles within the plant—no matter how good the cause—which, not infrequently, is given less prominence than the alluring list of prizes?

Lewis:

Gambling ought never to be an important part of a man's life. If it is a way in which large sums of money are transferred from person to person without doing any good (e.g., producing employment, goodwill, etc.) then it is a bad thing. If it is carried out on a small scale, I am not sure that it is bad. I don't know much about it, because it is about the only vice to which I have no temptation at all, and I think it is a risk to talk about things which are not in my own makeup, because I don't understand them. If anyone comes to me asking to play bridge for money, I just say: "How much do you hope to win? Take it and go away."

Question 14.

Many people are quite unable to understand the theological differences which have caused divisions in the Christian Church.

Do you consider that these differences are fundamental, and is the time now ripe for reunion?

Lewis:

The time is always ripe for reunion. Divisions between Christians are a sin and a scandal, and Christians ought at all times to be making contributions toward reunion, if it is only by their prayers. I am only a layman and a recent Christian, and I do not know much about these things, but in all the things which I have written and thought I have always stuck to traditional, dogmatic positions. The result is that letters of agreement reach me from what are ordinarily regarded as the most different kinds of Christians; for instance, I get letters from Jesuits, monks, nuns, and also from Quakers and Welsh Dissenters, and so on. So it seems to me that the "extremist" elements in every church are nearest one another and the liberal and "broad-minded" people in each body could never be united at all. The world of dogmatic Christianity is a place in which thousands of people of quite different types keep on saying the same thing, and the world of "broad-mindedness" and watered-down "religion" is a world where a small number of people (all of the same type) say totally different things and change their minds every few minutes. We shall never get reunion from them.

Question 15.

In the past the church used various kinds of compulsion in attempts to force a particular brand of Christianity on the community. Given sufficient power, is there not a danger of this sort of thing happening again?

Lewis:

Yes, I hear nasty rumors coming from Spain. Persecution is a temptation to which all men are exposed. I had a postcard signed "M. D." saying that anyone who expressed and published his belief in the Virgin Birth should be stripped and flogged. That shows you how easily persecution of Christians by the non-Christians might come back. Of course, they wouldn't call it persecution: they'd call it "compulsory reeducation of the ideologically unfit," or something like that. But, of course, I have to admit that Christians themselves have been persecutors in the past. It was worse of them, because *they* ought to have known better: they weren't worse in any other way. I detest every kind of religious compulsion: only the other day I was writing an angry letter to *The Spectator* about church parades in the Home Guard!

Question 16.

Is attendance at a place of worship or membership with a Christian community necessary to a Christian way of life?

Lewis:

That's a question which I cannot answer. My own experience is that when I first became a Christian, about fourteen years ago, I thought that I could do it on my own, by retiring to my rooms and reading theology, and I wouldn't go to the churches and Gospel halls; and then later I found that it was the only way of flying your flag; and, of course, I found that this meant being a target. It is extraordinary how inconvenient to your family it becomes for you to get up early to go to church. It doesn't matter so much if you get up early for anything else, but if you get up early to go to church it's very selfish of you and you upset the house. If there is anything in the teaching of the New Testament which is in the nature of a command, it is that you are obliged to take the Sacrament,[7] and you can't do it without going to church. I disliked very much their hymns, which I considered to be fifth-rate poems set to sixth-rate music. But as I went on I saw the great merit of it. I came up against different people of quite different outlooks and different education, and then gradually my conceit just began peeling off. I realized that the hymns (which were just sixth-rate music) were, nevertheless, being sung with devotion and benefit by an old saint in elastic-side boots in the opposite pew, and then you realize that you aren't fit to clean those boots. It gets you out of your solitary conceit. It is not for me to lay down laws, as I am only a layman, and I don't know much.

Question 17.

If it is true that one has only to want God enough in order

[7]John vi. 53-54: "Except ye eat the flesh of the Son of man, and drink his blood, ye have no life in you. Whoso eateth my flesh, and drinketh my blood, hath eternal life; and I will raise him up at the last day."

to find Him, how can I make myself want Him enough to enable myself to find Him?

Lewis:

If you don't want God, why are you so anxious to want to want Him? I think that in reality the want is a real one, and I should say that this person has in fact found God, although it may not be fully recognized yet. We are not always aware of things at the time they happen. At any rate, what is more important is that God has found this person, and that is the main thing.

4.

MYTH BECAME FACT

MY FRIEND CORINEUS HAS ADVANCED THE CHARGE THAT none of us are in fact Christians at all. According to him historic Christianity is something so barbarous that no modern man can really believe it: the moderns who claim to do so are in fact believing a modern system of thought which retains the vocabulary of Christianity and exploits the emotions inherited from it while quietly dropping its essential doctrines. Corineus compared modern Christianity with the modern English monarchy: the forms of kingship have been retained, but the reality has been abandoned.

All this I believe to be false, except of a few "modernist" theologians who, by God's grace, become fewer every day. But for the moment let us assume that Corineus is right. Let us pretend, for purposes of argument, that *all* who now call themselves Christians have abandoned the historic doctrines. Let us suppose that modern "Christianity" reveals a system of names, ritual, formulae, and metaphors which persists although the thoughts behind it have changed. Corineus ought to be able to *explain* the persistence.

Why, on his view, do all these educated and enlightened pseudo-Christians insist on expressing their deepest thoughts in terms of an archaic mythology which must hamper and embarrass them at every turn? Why do they refuse to cut the umbilical cord which binds the living and flourishing child to its moribund mother? For, if Corineus is right, it should be a great relief to them to do so. Yet the odd thing is that even those who seem most embarrassed by the sediment of "barbaric" Christianity in their thought become suddenly obstinate when you ask them to get rid of it altogether. They will strain the cord almost to breaking point, but they refuse to cut it. Sometimes they will take every step except the last one.

If all who professed Christianity were clergymen, it would

be easy (though uncharitable) to reply that their livelihood depends on *not* taking that last step. Yet even if this were the true cause of their behavior, even if all clergymen are intellectual prostitutes who preach for pay—and usually starvation pay—what they secretly believe to be false, surely so widespread a darkening of conscience among thousands of men not otherwise known to be criminal, itself demands explanation? And of couse the profession of Christianity is not confined to the clergy. It is professed by millions of women and laymen who earn thereby contempt, unpopularity, suspicion, and the hostility of their own families. How does this come to happen?

Obstinacies of this sort are interesting. "Why not cut the cord?" asks Corineus. "Everything would be much easier if you would free your thought from this vestigial mythology." To be sure: far easier. Life would be far easier for the mother of an invalid child if she put it into an institution and adopted someone else's healthy baby instead. Life would be far easier to many a man if he abandoned the woman he has actually fallen in love with and married someone else because she is more suitable. The only defect of the healthy baby and the suitable woman is that they leave out the patient's only reason for bothering about a child or wife at all. "Would not conversation be much more rational than dancing?" said Jane Austen's Miss Bingley. "Much more rational," replied Mr. Bingley, "but much less like a ball."[1]

In the same way, it would be much more rational to abolish the English monarchy. But how if, by doing so, you leave out the one element in our state which matters most? How if the monarchy is the channel through which all the *vital* elements of citizenship—loyalty, the consecration of secular life, the hierarchical principle, splendor, ceremony, continuity—still trickle down to irrigate the dust bowl of modern economic statecraft?

The real answer of even the most "modernist" Christianity to Corineus is the same. Even assuming (which I most constantly deny) that the doctrines of historic Christianity are merely mythical, it is the myth which is the vital and nourishing element in the whole concern. Corineus wants us to move with the times. Now, we know where times move. They move *away*. But in religion we find something that does not move away. It is what Corineus calls the myth, that abides; it is what

[1] *Pride and Prejudice*, ch. xi.

calls the modern and living thought that moves away. Not only the thought of theologians, but the thought of antitheologians. Where are the predecessors of Corineus? Where is the epicureanism of Lucretius,[2] the pagan revival of Julian the Apostate?[3] Where are the Gnostics, where is the monism of Averroës,[4] the deism of Voltaire, the dogmatic materialism of the great Victorians? They have moved with the times. But the thing they were all attacking remains: Corineus finds it still there to attack. The myth (to speak his language) has outlived the thoughts of all its defenders and of all its adversaries. It is the myth that gives life. Those elements even in modernist Christianity which Corineus regards as vestigial, are the substance: what he takes for the "real modern belief" is the shadow.

To explain this we must look a little closer at myth in general, and at this myth in particular. Human intellect is incurably abstract. Pure mathematics is the type of successful thought. Yet the only realities we experience are concrete—this pain, this pleasure, this dog, this man. While we are loving the man, bearing the pain, enjoying the pleasure, we are not intellectually apprehending Pleasure, Pain or Personality. When we begin to do so, on the other hand, the concrete realities sink to the level of mere instances or examples: we are no longer dealing with them, but with that which they exemplify. This is our dilemma—either to taste and not to know or to know and not to taste—or, more strictly, to lack one kind of knowledge because we are in an experience or to lack another kind because we are outside it. As thinkers we are cut off from what we think about; as tasting, touching, willing, loving, hating, we do not clearly understand. The more lucidly we think, the more we are cut off: the more deeply we enter into reality, the less we can think. You cannot *study* pleasure in the moment of the nuptial embrace, nor repentance while repenting, nor analyze the nature of humor while roaring with laughter. But when else can you really know these things? "If only my toothache would stop, I could write another chapter about pain." But once it stops, what do I know about pain?

Of this tragic dilemma myth is the partial solution. In the

[2]Titus Lucretius Carus (c. 99–55), the Roman poet.

[3]Roman emperor, A.D. 361–3.

[4]Averroës (1126–98), of Cordova, believed that only one intellect exists for the whole human race in which every individual participates, to the exclusion of personal immortality.

enjoyment of a great myth we come nearest to experiencing as a concrete what can otherwise be understood only as an abstraction. At this moment, for example, I am trying to understand something very abstract indeed—the fading, vanishing of tasted reality as we try to grasp it with the discursive reason. Probably I have made heavy weather of it. But if I remind you, instead, of Orpheus and Eurydice, how he was suffered to lead her by the hand but, when he turned round to look at her, she disappeared, what was merely a principle becomes imaginable. You may reply that you never till this moment attached that "meaning" to that myth. Of course not. You are not looking for an abstract "meaning" at all. If that was what you were doing, the myth would be for you no true myth but a mere allegory. You were not knowing, but tasting; but what you were tasting turns out to be a universal principle. The moment we *state* this principle, we are admittedly back in the world of abstraction. It is only while receiving the myth as a story that you experience the principle concretely.

When we translate we get abstraction—or rather, dozens of abstractions. What flows into you from the myth is not truth but reality (truth is always *about* something, but reality is that *about which* truth is), and, therefore, every myth becomes the father of innumerable truths on the abstract level. Myth is the mountain whence all the different streams arise which become truths down here in the valley; *in hac valle abstractionis.*[5] Or, if you prefer, myth is the isthmus which connects the peninsular world of thought with that vast continent we really belong to. It is not, like truth, abstract; nor is it, like direct experience, bound to the particular.

Now as myth transcends thought, incarnation transcends myth. The heart of Christianity is a myth which is also a fact. The old myth of the dying god, *without ceasing to be myth,* comes down from the heaven of legend and imagination to the earth of history. It *happens*—at a particular date, in a particular place, followed by definable historical consequences. We pass from a Balder or an Osiris, dying nobody knows when or where, to a historical person crucified (it is all in order) *under Pontius Pilate*. By becoming fact it does not cease to be myth: that is the miracle. I suspect that men have sometimes derived more spiritual sustenance from myths they did not believe than from the religion they professed. To be truly Christian we must both

[5] "In this valley of separation."

assent to the historical fact and also receive the myth (fact though it has become) with the same imaginative embrace which we accord to all myths. The one is hardly more necessary than the other.

A man who disbelieved the Christian story as fact but continually fed on it as myth would, perhaps, be more spiritually alive than one who assented and did not think much about it. The modernist—the extreme modernist, infidel in all but name—need not be called a fool or hypocrite because he obstinately retains, even in the midst of his intellectual atheism, the language, rites, sacraments, and story of the Christians. The poor man may be clinging (with a wisdom he himself by no means understands) to that which is his life. It would have been better that Loisy[6] should have remained a Christian: it would not necessarily have been better that he should have purged his thought of vestigial Christianity.

Those who do not know that this great myth became fact when the Virgin conceived are, indeed, to be pitied. But Christians also need to be reminded—we may thank Corineus for reminding us—that what became fact was a myth, that it carries with it into the world of fact all the properties of a myth. God is more than a god, not less; Christ is more than Balder, not less. We must not be ashamed of the mythical radiance resting on our theology. We must not be nervous about "parallels" and "pagan Christs": they *ought* to be there—it would be a stumbling block if they weren't. We must not, in false spirituality, withhold our imaginative welcome. If God chooses to be mythopoeic—and is not the sky itself a myth—shall we refuse to be *mythopathic?* For this is the marriage of heaven and earth: perfect myth and perfect fact: claiming not only our love and our obedience, but also our wonder and delight, addressed to the savage, the child, and the poet in each one of us no less than to the moralist, the scholar, and the philosopher.

[6]Alfred Loisy (1857–1940), a French theologian and founder of the Modernist Movement.

5 .

"HORRID RED THINGS"

MANY THEOLOGIANS AND SOME SCIENTISTS ARE NOW READY to proclaim that the nineteenth century "conflict between science and religion" is over and done with. But even if this is true, it is a truth known only to real theologians and real scientists—that is, to a few highly educated men. To the man in the street the conflict is still perfectly real, and in his mind it takes a form which the learned hardly dream of.

The ordinary man is not thinking of particular dogmas and particular scientific discoveries. What troubles him is an all-pervading difference of atmosphere between what he believes Christianity to be and that general picture of the universe which he has picked up from living in a scientific age. He gathers from the Creed that God has a "Son" (just as if God were a god, like Odin or Jupiter): that this Son "came down" (like a parachutist) from "Heaven," first to earth and later to some land of the dead situated beneath the earth's surface: that, still later, He ascended into the sky and took His seat in a decorated chair placed a little to the right of His Father's throne. The whole thing seems to imply a local and material heaven—a palace in the stratosphere—a flat earth and all the rest of those archaic misconceptions.

The ordinary man is well aware that we should deny all the beliefs he attributes to us and interpret our creed in a different sense. But this by no means satisfies him. "No doubt," he thinks, "once those articles of belief are there, they can be allegorized or spiritualized away to any extent you please. But is it not plain that they would never have been there at all if the first generation of Christians had had any notion of what the real universe is like? A historian who has based his work on the misreading of a document may afterwards (when his mistake has been exposed) exercise great ingenuity in showing that his account of a certain battle can still be reconciled with

43

what the document records. But the point is that none of these ingenious explanations would ever have come into existence if he had read his documents correctly at the outset. They are therefore really a waste of labor; it would be manlier of him to admit his mistake and begin all over again."

I think there are two things that Christians must do if they wish to convince this "ordinary" modern man. In the first place, they must make it quite clear that what will remain of the Creed after all their explanations and reinterpretations will still be something quite unambiguously supernatural, miraculous, and shocking. We may not believe in a flat earth and a sky palace. But we must insist from the beginning that we believe, as firmly as any savage or theosophist, in a spirit world which can, and does, invade the natural or phenomenal universe. For the plain man suspects that when we start explaining, we are going to explain away: that we have mythology for our ignorant hearers and are ready, when cornered by educated hearers, to reduce it to innocuous moral platitudes which no one ever dreamed of denying. And there are theologians who justify this suspicion. From them we must part company absolutely. If nothing remains except what could be equally well stated without Christian formulae, then the honest thing is to admit that Christianity is untrue and to begin over again without it.

In the second place, we must try to teach something about the difference between thinking and imagining. It is, of course, an historical error to suppose that all, or even most, early Christians believed in the sky palace in the same sense in which we believe in the solar system. Anthropomorphism was condemned by the church as soon as the question was explicitly before her. But some early Christians may have done this; and probably thousands never thought of their faith without anthropomorphic imagery. That is why we must distinguish the core of belief from the attendant imagining.

When I think of London I always see a picture of Euston Station. But I do not believe that London *is* Euston Station. That is a simple case, because there the thinker *knows* the imagery to be false. Now let us take a more complex one. I once heard a lady tell her daughter that if you ate too many aspirin tablets you would die. "But why?" asked the child. "If you squash them you don't find any horrid red things inside them." Obviously, when this child thought of poison she not only had an attendant image of "horrid red things," but she actually believed that poison was red. And this is an error. But how far does it invalidate her thinking about poison? She learned that an overdose of aspirin would kill you; her belief was true. She knew, within limits, which of the substances in her mother's house were poisonous. If I, staying in the house, had raised a glass of what looked like water to my lips, and the child had said, "Don't drink that. Mummie says it's poisonous," I should have been foolish to disregard the warning on the ground that "This child has an archaic and mythological idea of poison as horrid red things."

There is thus a distinction not only between thought and imagination in general, but even between thought and those images which the thinker (falsely) believes to be true. When the child learned later that poison is not always red, she would not have felt that anything essential in her beliefs about poison had been altered. She would still know, as she had always known, that poison is what kills you if you swallow it. That is the essence of poison. The erroneous beliefs about color drop away without affecting it.

In the same way an early peasant Christian might have thought that Christ's sitting at the right hand of the Father really implied two chairs of state, in a certain spatial relation, inside a sky palace. But if the same man afterwards received a philosophical education and discovered that God has no body, parts, or passions, and therefore neither a right hand nor a palace, he would not have felt that the essentials of his belief had been altered. What had mattered to him, even in the days of his simplicity, had not been supposed details about celestial furniture. It had been the assurance that the once-crucified Master was now the supreme Agent or the unimaginable power on whom the whole universe depends. And he would recognize that in this he had never been deceived.

The critic may still ask us why the imagery—which we admit to be untrue—should be used at all. But he has not noticed that any language we attempt to substitute for it would involve imagery that is open to all the same objections. To say that God "enters" the natural order involves just as much spatial imagery as to say that He "comes down"; one has simply substituted horizontal (or undefined) for vertical movement. To say that He is "reabsorbed" into the noumenal is better than to say He "ascended" into heaven, only if the picture of something dissolving in warm fluid, or being sucked into a throat, is less misleading than the picture of a bird, or a balloon, going up. All language, except about objects of sense, is metaphorical through and through. To call God a "force" (that is, something like a wind or a dynamo) is as metaphorical as to call Him a father or a king. On such matters we can make our language more polysyllabic and duller: we cannot make it more literal. The difficulty is not peculiar to theologians. Scientists, poets, psychoanalysts, and metaphysicians are all in the same boat—

Man's reason is in such deep insolvency to sense.

Where, then, do we draw the line between explaining and "explaining away"? I do not think there is much difficulty. All that concerns the unincarnate activities of God—His operation on that plane of being where sense cannot enter—must be taken along with imagery which we know to be, in the literal sense, untrue. But there can be no defense for applying the same treatment to the miracles of the Incarnate God. They are recorded as events on this earth which affected human senses. They are the sort of thing we can describe literally. If Christ turned water into wine, and we had been present, we could have seen, smelled, and tasted. The story that He did so is not of the same order as His "sitting at the right hand of the Father." It is either fact, or legend, or lie. You must take it or leave it.

6.

RELIGION AND SCIENCE

Miracles," said my friend. "Oh, come. Science has knocked the bottom out of all that. We know that Nature is governed by fixed laws."

"Didn't people always know that?" said I.

"Good Lord, no," said he. "For instance, take a story like the Virgin Birth. We know now that such a thing couldn't happen. We know there *must* be a male spermatozoon."

"But look here," said I, "St. Joseph—"

"Who's he?" asked my friend.

"He was the husband of the Virgin Mary. If you'll read the story in the Bible you'll find that when he saw his fiancée was going to have a baby he decided to cry off the marriage. Why did he do that?"

"Wouldn't most men?"

"Any man would," said I, "provided he knew the Laws of Nature—in other words, provided he knew that a girl doesn't ordinarily have a baby unless she's been sleeping with a man. But according to your theory people in the old days didn't know that Nature was governed by fixed laws. I'm pointing out that the story shows that St. Joseph knew *that* law just as well as you do."

"But he came to believe in the Virgin Birth afterwards, didn't he?"

"Quite. But he didn't do so because he was under any illusion as to where babies came from in the ordinary course of Nature. He believed in the Virgin Birth as something *super*natural. He knew Nature works in fixed, regular ways: but he also believed that there existed something *beyond* Nature which could interfere with her workings—from outside, so to speak."

"But modern science has shown there's no such thing."

"Really," said I. "Which of the sciences?"

"Oh, well, that's a matter of detail," said my friend. "I can't give you chapter and verse from memory."

"But, don't you see," said I, "that science never could show anything of the sort?"

"Why on earth not?"

"Because science studies Nature. And the question is whether anything *besides* Nature exists—anything 'outside.' How could you find that out by studying simply Nature?"

"But don't we find out that Nature *must* work in an absolutely fixed way? I mean, the Laws of Nature tell us not merely how things *do* happen, but how they *must* happen. No power could possibly alter them."

"How do you mean?" said I.

"Look here," said he. "Could this 'something outside' that you talk about make two and two five?"

"Well, no," said I.

"All right," said he. "Well, I think the Laws of Nature are really like two and two making four. The idea of their being altered is as absurd as the idea of altering the laws of arithmetic."

"Half a moment," said I. "Suppose you put sixpence into a drawer today, and sixpence into the same drawer tomorrow. Do the laws of arithmetic make it certain you'll find a shilling's worth there the day after?"

"Of course," said he, "provided no one's been tampering with your drawer."

"Ah, but that's the whole point," said I. "The laws of arithmetic can tell you what you'll find, with absolute certainty, *provided that* there's no interference. If a thief has been at the drawer of course you'll get a different result. But the thief won't have broken the laws of arithmetic—only the laws of England. Now, aren't the Laws of Nature much in the same boat? Don't they all tell you what will happen *provided* there's no interference?"

"How do you mean?"

"Well, the laws will tell you how a billiard ball will travel on a smooth surface if you hit it in a particular way—but only provided no one interferes. If, after it's already in motion, someone snatches up a cue and gives it a biff on one side—why, then, you won't get what the scientist predicted."

"No, of course not. He can't allow for monkey tricks like that."

"Quite, and in the same way, if there was anything outside

Nature, and if it interfered—then the events which the scientist expected wouldn't follow. That would be what we call a miracle. In one sense it wouldn't break the laws of Nature. The laws tell you what will happen if nothing interferes. They can't tell you whether something *is* going to interfere. I mean, it's not the expert at arithmetic who can tell you how likely someone is to interfere with the pennies in my drawer; a detective would be more use. It isn't the physicist who can tell you how likely I am to catch up a cue and spoil his experiment with the billiard ball; you'd better ask a psychologist. And it isn't the scientist who can tell you how likely Nature is to be interfered with from outside. You must go to the metaphysician."

"These are rather niggling points," said my friend. "You see, the real objection goes far deeper. The whole picture of the universe which science has given us makes it such rot to believe that the power at the back of it all could be interested in us tiny little creatures crawling about on an unimportant planet! It was all so obviously invented by people who believed in a flat earth with the stars only a mile or two away."

"When did people believe that?"

"Why, all those old Christian chaps you're always telling about did. I mean Boethius and Augustine and Thomas Aquinas and Dante."

"Sorry," said I, "but this is one of the few subjects I do know something about."

I reached out my hand to a bookshelf. "You see this book," I said, "Ptolemy's *Almagest*. You know what it is?"

"Yes," said he. "It's the standard astronomical handbook used all through the Middle Ages."

"Well, just read that," I said, pointing to Book I, chapter 5.

"The earth," read out my friend, hesitating a bit as he translated the Latin, "the earth, in relation to the distance of the fixed stars, has no appreciable size and must be treated as a mathematical point!"

There was a moment's silence.

"Did they really know that *then?*" said my friend. "But—but none of the histories of science—none of the modern encyclopedias—ever mention the fact."

"Exactly," said I. "I'll leave you to think out the reason. It almost looks as if someone was anxious to hush it up, doesn't it? I wonder why."

There was another short silence.

"At any rate," said I, "we can now state the problem accurately. People usually think the problem is how to reconcile what we now know about the size of the universe with our traditional ideas of religion. That turns out not to be the problem at all. The real problem is this. The enormous size of the universe and the insignificance of the earth were known for centuries, and no one ever dreamed that they had any bearing on the religious question. Then, less than a hundred years ago, they are suddenly trotted out as an argument against Christianity. And the people who trot them out carefully hush up the fact that they were known long ago. Don't you think that all you atheists are strangely unsuspicious people?"

7.

THE LAWS OF NATURE

"POOR WOMAN," SAID MY FRIEND. "ONE HARDLY KNOWS WHAT to say when they talk like that. She thinks her son survived Arnhem because she prayed for him. It would be heartless to explain to her that he really survived because he was standing a little to the left or a little to the right of some bullet. That bullet was following a course laid down by the Laws of Nature. It couldn't have hit him. He just happened to be standing off its line . . . and so all day long as regards every bullet and every splinter of shell. His survival was simply due to the Laws of Nature."

At that moment my first pupil came in and the conversation was cut short, but later in the day I had to walk across the park to a committee meeting and this gave me time to think the matter over. It was quite clear that once a bullet had been fired from Point A in direction B, the wind being C, and so forth, it would pursue a certain path. But might our young friend have been standing somewhere else? And might the German have fired at a different moment or in a different direction? If men have free will it would appear that they might. On that view we get a rather more complicated picture of the battle of Arnhem. The total course of events would be a kind of amalgam derived from two sources—on the one hand, from acts of human will (which might presumably have been otherwise), and on the other, from the laws of physical nature. And this would seem to provide all that is necessary for the mother's belief that her prayers had some place among the causes of her son's preservation. God might continually influence the wills of all the combatants so as to allot death, wounds, and survival in the way He thought best, while leaving the behavior of the projectile to follow its normal course.

But I was still not quite clear about the physical side of this picture. I had been thinking (vaguely enough) that the bullet's

51

flight was *caused* by the Laws of Nature. But is this really so? Granted that the bullet is set in motion, and granted the wind and the earth's gravitation and all the other relevant factors, then it is a "Law" of Nature that the bullet must take the course it did. But then the pressing of the trigger, the side wind, and even the earth, are not exactly *laws*. They are facts or events. They are not laws but things that obey laws. Obviously, to consider the pressing of the trigger would only lead us back to the free-will side of the picture. We must, therefore, choose a simpler example.

The laws of physics, I understand, decree that when one billiard ball (A) sets another billiard ball (B) in motion, the momentum lost by A exactly equals the momentum gained by B. This is a *law*. That is, this is the pattern to which the movement of the two billiard balls must conform. Provided, of course, that something sets ball A in motion. And here comes the snag. The *law* won't set it in motion. It is usually a man with a cue who does that. But a man with a cue would send us back to free will, so let us assume that it was lying on a table in a liner and that what set it in motion was a lurch of the ship. In that case it was not the law which produced the movement; it was a wave. And that wave, though it certainly moved *according* to the laws of physics, was not moved by them. It was shoved by other waves, and by winds, and so forth. And however far you traced the story back you would never find *Laws* of Nature causing anything.

The dazzlingly obvious conclusion now arose in my mind: *in the whole history of the universe the Laws of Nature have never produced a single event*. They are the pattern to which every event must conform, provided only that it can be induced to happen. But how do you get it to do that? How do you get a move on? The Laws of Nature can give you no help there. All events obey them, just as all operations with money obey the laws of arithmetic. Add six pennies to six and the result will certainly be a shilling. But arithmetic by itself won't put one farthing into your pocket. Up till now I had had a vague idea that the Laws of Nature could make things happen. I now saw that this was exactly like thinking that you could increase your income by doing sums about it. The *laws* are the pattern to which events conform: the source of events must be sought elsewhere.

This may be put in the form that the Laws of Nature explain everything except the source of events. But this is rather a formidable exception. The laws, in one sense, cover the whole of reality except—well, except that continuous cataract of real events which makes up the actual universe. They explain everything except what we should ordinarily call "everything." The only thing they omit is—the whole universe. I do not mean that a knowledge of these laws is useless. Provided we can take over the actual universe as a going concern, such knowledge is useful and indeed indispensable for manipulating it; just as, if only you have some money arithmetic is indispensable for managing it. But the events themselves, the money itself—that is quite another affair.

Where, then, do actual events come from? In one sense the answer is easy. Each event comes from a previous event. But what happens if you trace this process backwards? To ask this is not exactly the same as to ask where *things* come from—how there came to be space and time and matter at all. Our present problem is not about things but about events; not, for example, about particles of matter but about this particle colliding with that. The mind can perhaps acquiesce in the idea that the "properties" of the universal drama somehow "just happen to be there": but whence comes the play, the story?

Either the stream of events had a beginning or it had not. If it had, then we are faced with something like creation. If it had not (a supposition, by the way, which some physicists find difficult), then we are faced with an everlasting impulse which, by its very nature, is opaque to scientific thought. Science, when it becomes perfect, will have explained the connection between each link in the chain and the link before it. But the actual existence of the chain will remain wholly unaccountable. We learn more and more about the pattern. We learn nothing about that which "feeds" real events into the pattern. If it is not God, we must at the very least call it destiny—the immaterial, ultimate, one-way pressure which keeps the universe on the move.

The smallest event, then, if we face the fact that it occurs (instead of concentrating on the pattern into which, if it can be persuaded to occur, it must fit), leads us back to a mystery which lies outside natural science. It is certainly a possible supposition that behind this mystery some mighty will and life is at work. If so, any contrast between His acts and the Laws of Nature is out of the question. It is His act alone that gives the laws any events to apply to. The laws are an empty frame; it is He who fills that frame—not now and then on specially "providential" occasions, but at every moment. And He, from His vantage point above time, can, if He pleases, take all prayers into account in ordaining that vast complex event which is the history of the universe. For what we call "future" prayers have always been present to Him.

In *Hamlet* a branch breaks and Ophelia is drowned. Did she die because the branch broke or because Shakespeare wanted her to die at that point in the play? Either— both—whichever you please. The alternative suggested by the question is not a real alternative at all—once you have grasped that Shakespeare is making the whole play.

8.

THE GRAND MIRACLE

ONE IS VERY OFTEN ASKED AT PRESENT WHETHER WE could not have a Christianity stripped, or, as people who ask it say, "freed" from its miraculous elements, a Christianity with the miraculous elements suppressed. Now, it seems to me that precisely the one religion in the world, or at least the only one I know, with which you could not do that is Christianity. In a religion like Buddhism, if you took away the miracles attributed to Gautama Buddha in some very late sources, there would be no loss; in fact, the religion would get on very much better without them because in that case the miracles largely contradict the teaching. Or even in the case of a religion like Mohammedanism, nothing essential would be altered if you took away the miracles. You could have a great prophet preaching his dogmas without bringing in any miracles; they are only in the nature of a digression, or illuminated capitals. But you cannot possibly do that with Christianity, because the Christian story is precisely the story of one grand miracle, the Christian assertion being that what is beyond all space and time, which is uncreated, eternal, came into Nature, into human nature, descended into His own universe, and rose again, bringing Nature up with Him. It is precisely one great miracle. If you take that away there is nothing specifically Christian left. There may be many admirable human things which Christianity shares with all other systems in the world, but there would be nothing specifically Christian. Conversely, once you have accepted that, then you will see that all other well-established Christian miracles—because, of course, there are ill-established Christian miracles; there are Christian legends just as much as there are heathen legends, or modern journalistic legends—you will see that all the well-established Christian miracles are part of it, that they all either prepare for, or exhibit, or result from the Incarnation. Just as every natural event exhibits the total character of the natural universe at a particular point and space of time, so every miracle exhibits the character of the Incarnation.

Now, if one asks whether that central grand miracle in Christianity is itself probable or improbable, of course, quite clearly you cannot be applying Hume's kind of probability. You cannot mean a probability based on statistics according to which the more often a thing has happened, the more likely it is to happen again (the more often you get indigestion from eating a certain food, the more probable it is, if you eat it again, that you will again have indigestion). Certainly the Incarnation cannot be probable in that sense. It is of its very nature to have happened only once. But then it is of the very nature of the history of this world to have happened only once; and if the Incarnation happened at all, it is the central chapter of that history. It is improbable in the same way in which the whole of nature is improbable, because it is only there once, and will happen only once. So one must apply to it a quite different kind of standard.

I think we are rather in this position. Supposing you had before you a manuscript of some great work, either a symphony or a novel. There then comes to you a person, saying, "Here is a new bit of the manuscript that I found; it is the central passage of that symphony, or the central chapter of that novel. The text is incomplete without it. I have got the missing passage which is really the center of the whole work." The only thing you could do would be to put this new piece of the manuscript in that central position, and then see how it reacted on the whole of the rest of the work. If it constantly brought out new meanings from the whole of the rest of the work, if it made you notice things in the rest of the work which you had not noticed before, then I think you would decide that it was authentic. On the other hand, if it failed to do that, then, however attractive it was in itself, you would reject it.

Now, what is the missing chapter in this case, the chapter which Christians are offering? The story of the Incarnation is the story of a descent and resurrection. When I say "resurrection" here, I am not referring simply to the first few hours, or the first few weeks of the Resurrection. I am talking of this whole, huge pattern of descent, down, down, and then up again. What we ordinarily call the Resurrection being just, so to speak, the point at which it turns. Think what that descent is. The coming down, not only into humanity, but into those nine months which precede human birth, in which they tell us we all recapitulate strange prehuman, subhuman forms of life, and going lower still into being a corpse, a thing which, if this ascending movement had not begun, would presently have passed out of the organic altogether, and have gone back into the inorganic, as all corpses do. One has a picture of someone going right down and dredging the sea bottom. One has a picture of a strong man trying to lift a very big, complicated burden. He stoops down and gets himself right under it so that he himself disappears; and then he straightens his back and moves off with the whole thing swaying on his shoulders. Or else one has the picture of a diver, stripping off garment after garment, making himself naked, then flashing for a moment in the air, and then down through the green, and warm, and sunlit water into the pitch-black, cold, freezing water, down into the mud and slime, then up again, his lungs almost bursting, back again to the green and warm and sunlit water, and then at last out into the sunshine, holding in his hand the dripping thing he went down to get. This thing is human nature; but, associated with it, all Nature, the new universe. That indeed is a point I cannot go into tonight, because it would take a whole sermon—this connection between human nature and Nature in general. It sounds startling, but I believe it can be fully justified.

Now, as soon as you have thought of this, this pattern of the huge dive down to the bottom, into the depths of the universe and coming up again into the light, everyone will see at once how that is imitated and echoed by the principles of the natural world; the descent of the seed into the soil, and its rising again in the plants. There are also all sorts of things in our own spiritual life where a thing has to be killed, and broken, in order that it may then become bright, and strong, and splendid. The analogy is obvious. In that sense the doctrine fits in very well, so well in fact that immediately there comes the suspicion, Is it not fitting in a great deal too well? In other words, does not the Christian story show this pattern of descent and reascent because that is part of all the nature religions of the world? We have read about it in *The Golden Bough*.[1] We all know about Adonis, and the stories of the rest of those rather tedious people; is not this one more instance of the same thing, "the dying god"? Well, yes it is. That is what makes the question subtle. What the anthropological critic of Chris-

---

[1] By Sir James George Frazer.

tianity is always saying is perfectly true. Christ *is* a figure of that sort. And here comes a very curious thing. When I first, after childhood, read the Gospels, I was full of that stuff about the dying god, *The Golden Bough*, and so on. It was to me then a very poetic, and mysterious, and quickening idea; and when I turned to the Gospels never will I forget my disappointment and repulsion at finding hardly anything about it at all. The metaphor of the seed dropping into the ground in this connection occurs (I think) twice in the New Testament,[2] and for the rest hardly any notice is taken; it seemed to me extraordinary. You had a dying God, Who was always representative of the corn: you see Him holding the corn, that is, bread, in His hand, and saying, "This is My Body,"[3] and from my point of view, as I then was, He did not seem to realize what He was saying. Surely there, if anywhere, this connection between the Christian story and the corn must have come out; the whole context is crying out for it. But everything goes on as if the principal actor, and still more, those about Him, were totally ignorant of what they were doing. It is as if you got very good evidence concerning the sea serpent, but the men who brought this good evidence seemed never to have heard of sea serpents. Or to put it in another way, why was it that the only case of the "dying god" which might conceivably have been historical occurred among a people (and the only people in the whole Mediterranean world) who had not got any trace of this nature religion, and indeed seemed to know nothing about it? Why is it among *them* the thing suddenly appears to happen?

The principal actor, humanly speaking, hardly seems to know of the repercussions His words (and sufferings) would have in any pagan mind. Well, that is almost inexplicable, except on one hypothesis. How if the corn king is not mentioned in that book, because He is here of whom the corn king was an image? How if the representation is absent because here, at last, the thing represented is present? If the shadows are absent because the thing of which they were shadows is here? The corn itself is in its far-off way an imitation of the supernatural reality; the thing dying, and coming to life again, descending, and reascending beyond all Nature. The principle is there in Nature because it was first there in God Himself. Thus one is getting in behind the nature religions, and behind Nature to

[2]John xii. 24; I Corinthians xv. 36.

[3]Matthew xxvi. 26; Mark xiv. 22; Luke xxii. 19; I Corinthians xi. 24.

Someone Who is not explained by, but explains, not, indeed, the nature religions directly, but that whole characteristic behavior of Nature on which nature religions were based. Well, that is one way in which it surprised me. It seemed to fit in a very peculiar way, showing me something about Nature more fully than I had seen it before, while itself remaining quite outside and above the nature religions.

Then another thing. We, with our modern democratic and arithmetical presuppositions would so have liked and expected all men to start equal in their search for God. One has the picture of great centripetal roads coming from all directions, with well-disposed people, all meaning the same thing, and getting closer and closer together. How shockingly opposite to that is the Christian story! One people picked out of the whole earth; that people purged and proved again and again. Some are lost in the desert before they reach Palestine; some stay in Babylon; some becoming indifferent. The whole thing narrows and narrows, until at last it comes down to a little point, small as the point of a spear—a Jewish girl at her prayers. That is what the whole of human nature has narrowed down to before the Incarnation takes place. Very unlike what we expected, but, of course, not in the least unlike what seems, in general, as shown by Nature, to be God's way of working. The universe is quite a shockingly selective, undemocratic place out of apparently infinite space, a relatively tiny proportion occupied by matter of any kind. Of the stars perhaps only one has planets: of the planets only one is at all likely to sustain organic life. Of the animals only one species is rational. Selection as seen in Nature, and the appalling waste which it involves, appears a horrible and an unjust thing by human standards. But the selectiveness in the Christian story is not quite like that. The people who are selected are, in a sense, unfairly selected for a supreme honor; but it is also a supreme burden. The people of Israel come to realize that it is their woes which are saving the world. Even in human society, though, one sees how this inequality furnishes an opportunity for every kind of tyranny and servility. Yet, on the other hand, one also sees that it furnishes an opportunity for some of the very best things we can think of—humility, and kindness, and the immense pleasures of admiration. (I cannot conceive how one would get through the boredom of a world in which you never met anyone more clever, or more beautiful, or stronger than yourself. The very crowds who go after the football celebrities and film stars know better than to desire that kind of equality!) What the story of the Incarnation seems to be doing is to flash a new light on a principle in Nature, and to show for the first time that this principle of inequality in Nature is neither good nor bad. It is a common theme running through both the goodness and badness of the natural world, and I begin to see how it can survive as a supreme beauty in a redeemed universe.

And with that I have unconsciously passed over to the third point. I have said that the selectiveness was not unfair in the way in which we first suspect, because those selected for the great honor are also selected for the great suffering, and their suffering heals others. In the Incarnation we get, of course, this idea of vicariousness of one person profiting by the earning of another person. In its highest form that is the very center of Christianity. And we also find this same vicariousness to be a characteristic, or, as the musician would put it, a *leitmotif* of Nature. It is a law of the natural universe that no being can exist on its own resources. Everyone, everything, is hopelessly indebted to everyone and everything else. In the universe, as we now see it, this is the source of many of the greatest horrors: all the horrors of carnivorousness, and the worse horrors of the parasites, those horrible animals that live under the skin of other animals, and so on. And yet, suddenly seeing it in the light of the Christian story, one realizes that vicariousness is not in itself bad; that all these animals, and insects, and horrors are merely that principle of vicariousness twisted in one way. For when you think it out, nearly everything good in Nature also comes from vicariousness. After all, the child, both before and after birth, lives on its mother, just as the parasite lives on its host, the one being a horror, the other being the source of almost every natural goodness in the world. It all depends upon what you do with this principle. So that I find in that third way also, that what is implied by the Incarnation just fits in exactly with what I have seen in Nature, and (this is the important point) each time it gives it a new twist. If I accept this supposed missing chapter, the Incarnation, I find it begins to illuminate the whole of the rest of the manuscript. It lights up Nature's pattern of death and rebirth; and, secondly, her selectiveness; and, thirdly, her vicariousness.

Now I notice a very odd point. All other religions in the world, as far as I know them, are either nature religions, or antinature religions. The nature religions are those of the old, simple pagan sort that you know about. You actually got drunk

in the temple of Bacchus. You actually committed fornication
in the temple of Aphrodite. The more modern form of nature
religion would be the religion started, in a sense, by Bergson[4]
(but he repented, and died Christian), and carried on in a more
popular form by Mr. Bernard Shaw. The antinature religions
are those like Hinduism and Stoicism, where men say, "I will
starve my flesh. I care not whether I live or die." All natural
things are to be set aside: the aim is Nirvana, apathy, negative
spirituality. The nature religions simply affirm my natural desires. The antinatural religions simply contradict them. The
nature religions simply give a new sanction to what I already
always thought about the universe in my moments of rude health
and cheerful brutality. The antinature religions merely repeat
what I always thought about it in my moods of lassitude, or
delicacy, or compassion.

But here is something quite different. Here is something
telling me—well, what? Telling me that I must never, like the
Stoics, say that death does not matter. Nothing is less Christian
than that. Death which made Life Himself shed tears at the
grave of Lazarus,[5] and shed tears of blood in Gethsemane.[6]
This is an appalling horror; a stinking indignity. (You remember
Thomas Browne's splendid remark: "I am not so much afraid
of death, as ashamed of it.")[7] And yet, somehow or other,
infinitely good. Christianity does not simply affirm or simply
deny the horror of death; it tells me something quite new about
it. Again, it does not, like Nietzsche, simply confirm my desire
to be stronger, or cleverer than other people. On the other
hand, it does not allow me to say, "Oh, Lord, won't there be
a day when everyone will be as good as everyone else?" In the
same way, about vicariousness. It will not, in any way, allow
me to be an exploiter, to act as a parasite on other people; yet
it will not allow me any dream of living on my own. It will
teach me to accept with glad humility the enormous sacrifice
that others make for me, as well as to make sacrifices for others.

That is why I think this Grand Miracle is the missing chapter
in this novel, the chapter on which the whole plot turns; that

[4]Henri Bergson (1859–1941). His "nature religion" is particularly evident in his *Matière et Mémoire* (1896) and *L'Evolution Créatrice* (1907).
[5]John xi. 35.
[6]Luke xxii. 44.
[7]Browne's actual words are "I am not so much afraid of death, as
ashamed thereof." *Religio Medici*, First Part, Section 40.

is why I believe that God really has dived down into the bottom of creation, and has come up bringing the whole redeemed Nature on His shoulder. The miracles that have already happened are, of course, as Scripture so often says, the first fruits of that cosmic summer which is presently coming on.[8] Christ has risen, and so we shall rise. St. Peter for a few seconds walked on the water,[9] and the day will come when there will be a remade universe, infinitely obedient to the will of glorified and obedient men, when we can do all things, when we shall be those gods that we are described as being in Scripture. To be sure, it feels wintry enough still; but often in the very early spring it feels like that. Two thousand years are only a day or two by this scale. A man really ought to say, "The Resurrection happened two thousand years ago" in the same spirit in which he says, "I saw a crocus yesterday." Because we know what is coming behind the crocus. The spring comes slowly down this way; but the great thing is that the corner has been turned. There is, of course, this difference, that in the natural spring the crocus cannot choose whether it will respond or not. We can. We have the power either of withstanding the spring, and sinking back into the cosmic winter, or of going on into those "high midsummer pomps" in which our leader, the Son of man, already dwells, and to which He is calling us. It remains with us to follow or not, to die in this winter, or to go on into that spring and that summer.

[8]Romans viii. 23; xi. 16; xvi. 5; I Corinthians xv. 20; James i. 18; Revelation xiv. 4.
[9]Matthew xiv. 29.

9.

CHRISTIAN APOLOGETICS

SOME OF YOU ARE PRIESTS AND SOME ARE LEADERS OF youth organizations.[1] I have little right to address either. It is for priests to teach me, not for me to teach them. I have never helped to organize youth, and while I was young myself I successfully avoided being organized. If I address you it is in response to a request so urged that I came to regard compliance as a matter of obedience.

I am to talk about apologetics. Apologetics means of course defense. The first question is—what do you propose to defend? Christianity, of course: and Christianity as understood by the church in Wales. And here at the outset I must deal with an unpleasant business. It seems to the layman that in the Church of England we often hear from our priests doctrine which is not Anglican Christianity. It may depart from Anglican Christianity in either of two ways: (1) It may be so "broad" or "liberal" or "modern" that it in fact excludes any real supernaturalism and thus ceases to be Christian at all. (2) It may, on the other hand, be Roman. It is not, of course, for me to define to you what Anglican Christianity is—I am your pupil, not your teacher. But I insist that wherever you draw the lines, bounding lines must exist, beyond which your doctrine will cease either to be Anglican or to be Christian: and I suggest also that the lines come a great deal sooner than many modern priests think. I think it is your duty to fix the lines clearly in your own minds: and if you wish to go beyond them you must change your profession.

This is your duty not specially as Christians or as priests but as honest men. There is a danger here of the clergy developing a special professional conscience which obscures the

---

[1]This paper was read to an assembly of Anglican priests and youth leaders at the "Carmarthen Conference for Youth Leaders and Junior Clergy" of the Church in Wales at Carmarthen during Easter 1945.

very plain moral issue. Men who have passed beyond these boundary lines in either direction are apt to protest that they have come by their unorthodox opinions honestly. In defense of those opinions they are prepared to suffer obloquy and to forfeit professional advancement. They thus come to feel like martyrs. But this simply misses the point which so gravely scandalizes the layman. We never doubted that the unorthodox opinions were honestly held: what we complain of is your continuing your ministry after you have come to hold them. We always knew that a man who makes his living as a paid agent of the Conservative party may honestly change his views and honestly become a Communist. What we deny is that he can honestly continue to be a Conservative agent and to receive money from one party while he supports the policy of another.

Even when we have thus ruled out teaching which is in direct contradiction to our profession, we must define our task still further. We are to defend Christianity itself—the faith preached by the Apostles, attested by the Martyrs, embodied in the Creeds, expounded by the Fathers. This must be clearly distinguished from the whole of what any one of us may think about God and man. Each of us has his individual emphasis: each holds, in addition to the faith, many opinions which seem to him to be consistent with it and true and important. And so perhaps they are. But as apologists it is not our business to defend *them*. We are defending Christianity; not "my religion." When we mention our personal opinions we must always make quite clear the difference between them and the faith itself. St. Paul has given us the model in I Corinthians vii. 25: on a certain point he has "no commandment of the Lord" but gives "his judgment." No one is left in doubt as to the difference in *status* implied.

This distinction, which is demanded by honesty, also gives the apologist a great tactical advantage. The great difficulty is to get modern audiences to realize that you are preaching Christianity solely and simply because you happen to think it *true;* they always suppose you are preaching it because you like it or think it good for society or something of that sort. Now a clearly maintained distinction between what the faith actually says and what you would like it to have said or what you understand or what you personally find helpful or think probable, forces your audience to realize that you are tied to your data just as the scientist is tied by the results of the experiments; that you are not just saying what you like. This immediately helps them to realize that what is being discussed is a question about objective fact—not gas about ideals and points of view.

Secondly, this scrupulous care to preserve the Christian message as something distinct from one's own ideas, has one very good effect upon the apologist himself. It forces him, again and again, to face up to those elements in original Christianity which he personally finds obscure or repulsive. He is saved from the temptation to skip or slur or ignore what he finds disagreeable. And the man who yields to that temptation will, of course, never progress in Christian knowledge. For obviously the doctrines which one finds easy are the doctrines which give Christian sanction to truths you already knew. The new truth which you do not know and which you need must, in the very nature of things, be hidden precisely in the doctrines you least like and least understand. It is just the same here as in science. The phenomenon which is troublesome, which doesn't fit in with the current scientific theories, is the phenomenon which compels reconsideration and thus leads to new knowledge. Science progresses because scientists, instead of running away from such troublesome phenomena or hushing them up, are constantly seeking them out. In the same way, there will be progress in Christian knowledge only as long as we accept the challenge of the difficult or repellent doctrines. A "liberal" Christianity which considers itself free to alter the faith whenever the faith looks perplexing or repellent *must* be completely stagnant. Progress is made only into a *resisting* material.

From this there follows a corollary about the apologist's private reading. There are two questions he will naturally ask himself. (1) Have I been "keeping up," keeping abreast of recent movements in theology? (2) Have I *stood firm (super monstratas vias)*[2] amid all these "winds of doctrine"?[3] I want to say emphatically that the second question is far the more important of the two. Our upbringing and the whole atmosphere of the world we live in make it certain that our main temptation will be that of yielding to winds of doctrine, not that of ignoring them. We are not at all likely to be hidebound: we are very

[2]The source of this is, I believe, Jeremiah vi. 16: *"State super vias et videte, et interrogate de semitis antiquis quae sit via bona, et ambulate in ea"* which is translated "Stand ye in the ways, and see, and ask for the old paths, where is the good way, and walk therein."

[3]Ephesians iv. 14.

likely indeed to be the slaves of fashion. If one has to choose between reading the new books and reading the old, one must choose the old: not because they are necessarily better but because they contain precisely those truths of which our own age is neglectful. The standard of permanent Christianity must be kept clear in our minds and it is against that standard that we must test all contemporary thought. In fact, we must at all costs *not* move with the times. We serve One who said "Heaven and Earth shall move with the times, but my words shall not move with the times."[4]

I am speaking, so far, of theological reading. Scientific reading is a different matter. If you know any science it is very desirable that you should keep it up. We have to answer the current scientific attitude toward Christianity, not the attitude which scientists adopted one hundred years ago. Science is in continual change and we must try to keep abreast of *it*. For the same reason, we must be very cautious of snatching at any scientific theory which, for the moment, seems to be in our favor. We may *mention* such things; but we must mention them lightly and without claiming that they are more than "interesting." Sentences beginning "Science has now proved" should be avoided. If we try to base our apologetic on some recent development in science, we shall usually find that just as we have put the finishing touches to our argument science has changed its mind and quietly withdrawn the theory we have been using as our foundation stone. *Timeo Danaos et dona ferentes*[5] is a sound principle.

While we are on the subject of science, let me digress for a moment. I believe that any Christian who is qualified to write a good popular book on any science may do much more by that than by any directly apologetic work. The difficulty we are up against is this. We can make people (often) attend to the Christian point of view for half an hour or so; but the moment they have gone away from our lecture or laid down our article, they are plunged back into a world where the opposite position is taken for granted. As long as that situation exists, widespread success is simply impossible. We must attack the enemy's line of communication. What we want is not more little books about Christianity, but more little books by

---

[4]Matthew xxiv. 35; Mark xiii. 31; Luke xxi. 33.

[5]"I fear the Greeks even when they bear gifts," Virgil, *Aeneid*, bk. II, line 49.

Christians on other subjects—with their Christianity *latent*. You can see this most easily if you look at it the other way round. Our faith is not very likely to be shaken by any book on Hinduism. But if whenever we read an elementary book on Geology, Botany, Politics, or Astronomy, we found that its implications were Hindu, that would shake us. It is not the books written in direct defense of materialism that make the modern man a materialist; it is the materialistic assumptions in all the other books. In the same way, it is not books on Christianity that will really trouble him. But he would be troubled if, whenever he wanted a cheap popular introduction to some science, the best work on the market was always by a Christian. The first step to the reconversion of this country is a series, produced by Christians, which can beat the *Penguin* and the *Thinkers Library* on their own ground. Its Christianity would have to be latent, not explicit: and *of course* its science perfectly honest. Science *twisted* in the interests of apologetics would be sin and folly. But I must return to my immediate subject.

Our business is to present that which is timeless (the same yesterday, today, and tomorrow)[6] in the particular language of our own age. The bad preacher does exactly the opposite: he takes the ideas of our own age and tricks them out in the traditional language of Christianity. Thus, for example, he may think about the Beveridge Report[7] and *talk* about the coming of the Kingdom. The core of his thought is merely contemporary; only the superficies is traditional. But your teaching must be timeless at its heart and wear a modern dress.

This raises the question of theology and politics. The nearest I can get to a settlement of the frontier problem between them is this: that theology teaches us what ends are desirable and what means are lawful, while politics teaches what means are effective. Thus theology tells us that every man ought to have a decent wage. Politics tells by what means this is likely to be attained. Theology tells us which of these means are consistent with justice and charity. On the political question guidance comes not from revelation but from natural prudence, knowledge of complicated facts and ripe experience. If we have these

[6]Hebrews xiii. 8.

[7]Sir William H. Beveridge, *Social Insurance and Allied Services*, Command Paper 6404, Parliamentary Session 1942–43 (London: H. M. Stationery Office, 1942). The "Beveridge Report" is a plan for the present social security system in Britain.

qualifications we may, of course, state our political opinions: but then we must make it quite clear that we are giving our personal judgment and have no command from the Lord. Not many priests have these qualifications. Most political sermons teach the congregation nothing except what newspapers are taken at the rectory.

Our great danger at present is lest the church should continue to practice a merely missionary technique in what has become a missionary situation. A century ago our task was to edify those who had been brought up in the faith: our present task is chiefly to convert and instruct infidels. Great Britain is as much part of the mission field as China. Now if you were sent to the Bantus you would be taught their language and traditions. You need similar teaching about the language and mental habits of your own uneducated and unbelieving fellow countrymen. Many priests are quite ignorant on this subject. What I know about it I have learned from talking in R.A.F.[8] camps. They were mostly inhabited by Englishmen and, therefore, some of what I shall say may be irrelevant to the situation in Wales. You will sift out what does not apply.

(1) I find that the uneducated Englishman is an almost total sceptic about history. I had expected he would disbelieve the Gospels because they contain miracles: but he really disbelieves them because they deal with things that happened two thousand years ago. He would disbelieve equally in the battle of Actium if he heard of it. To those who have had our kind of education, his state of mind is very difficult to realize. To us the present has always appeared as one section in a huge continuous process. In his mind the present occupies almost the whole field of vision. Beyond it, isolated from it, and quite unimportant, is something called "the old days"—a small, comic jungle in which highwaymen, Queen Elizabeth, knights-in-armor, etc. wander about. Then (strangest of all) beyond the old days comes a picture of "primitive man." He is "science," not "history," and is therefore felt to be much more real than the old days. In other words, the prehistoric is much more believed in than the historic.

(2) He has a distrust (very rational in the state of his knowledge) of ancient texts. Thus a man has sometimes said to me, "These records were written in the days before printing, weren't they? And you haven't got the original bit of paper, have you?

---

[8]The Royal Air Force.

So what it comes to is that someone wrote something and someone else copied it and someone else copied *that* and so on. Well, by the time it comes to us, it won't be in the least like the original." This is a difficult objection to deal with because one cannot, there and then, start teaching the whole science of textual criticism. But at this point their real religion (i.e. faith in "science") has come to my aid. The assurance that there is a "science" called "textual criticism" and that its results (not only as regards the New Testament, but as regards ancient texts in general) are generally accepted, will usually be received without objection. (I need hardly point out that the word "text" must not be used, since to your audience it means only "a scriptural quotation.")

(3) A sense of sin is almost totally lacking. Our situation is thus very different from that of the Apostles. The Pagans (and still more the *metuentes*[9]) to whom they preached were haunted by a sense of guilt and to them the Gospel was, therefore, "good news." We address people who have been trained to believe that whatever goes wrong in the world is someone else's fault—the capitalists', the government's, the Nazis', the generals', etc. They approach God Himself as His *judges*. They want to know, not whether they can be acquitted for sin, but whether He can be acquitted for creating such a world.

In attacking this fatal insensibility it is useless to direct attention (a) To sins your audience do not commit, or (b) To things they do, but do not regard as sins. They are usually not drunkards. They are mostly fornicators, but then they do not feel fornication to be wrong. It is, therefore, useless to dwell on either of these subjects. (Now that contraceptives have removed the obviously *uncharitable* element in fornication I do not myself think we can expect people to recognize it as sin until they have accepted Christianity as a whole.)

I cannot offer you a watertight technique for awakening the sense of sin. I can only say that, in my experience, if one begins from the sin that has been one's own chief problem during the last week, one is very often surprised at the way this shaft goes home. But whatever method we use, our continual effort must be to get their mind away from public affairs and "crime" and bring them down to brass tacks—to the whole

[9]The *metuentes* or "god-fearers" were a class of Gentiles who worshiped God without submitting to circumcision and the other ceremonial obligations of the Jewish Law. See Psalm cxviii. 4 and Acts. x. 2.

network of spite, greed, envy, unfairness, and conceit in the lives of "ordinary decent people" like themselves (and ourselves).

(4) We must learn the language of our audience. And let me say at the outset that it is no use at all laying down *a priori* what the "plain man" does or does not understand. You have to find out by experience. Thus most of us would have supposed that the change from "may truly and indifferently minister justice" to "may truly and impartially"[10] made that place easier to the uneducated; but a priest of my acquaintance discovered that his sexton saw no difficulty in *indifferently* ("It means making no difference between one man and another," he said) but had no idea what *impartially* meant.

On this question of language the best thing I can do is to make a list of words which are used by the people in a sense different from ours.

ATONEMENT. Does not really exist in a spoken modern English, though it would be recognized as "a religious word." Insofar as it conveys any meaning to the uneducated I think it means *compensation*. No one word will express to them what Christians mean by *atonement*: you must paraphrase.

BEING. (Noun) Never means merely "entity" in popular speech. Often it means what we should call a "personal being" (e.g. a man said to me "I believe in the Holy Ghost but I don't think He is a being!").

CATHOLIC means papistical.

CHARITY. Means (a) Alms (b) A "charitable organization" (c) Much more rarely—indulgence (i.e. a "charitable" attitude toward a man is conceived as one that denies or condones his sins, not as one that loves the sinner in spite of them).

CHRISTIAN. Has come to include almost no idea of *belief*. Usually a vague term of approval. The question "What do you call a Christian?" has been asked of me again and again.

[10]The first quotation is from the prayer from the "Whole state of Christ's Church" in the service of Holy Communion, Prayer Book (1662). The second is the revised form of that same phrase as found in the 1928 Prayer Book.

The answer they *wish* to receive is "A Christian is a decent chap who's unselfish, etc."

CHURCH. Means (a) A sacred building, (b) The clergy. Does *not* suggest to them the "company of all faithful people."[11] Generally used in a bad sense. Direct defense of the church is part of our duty; but use of the word *church* where there is no time to defend it alienates sympathy and should be avoided where possible.

CREATIVE. Now means merely "talented," "original." The idea of creation in the theological sense is absent from their minds.

CREATURE means "beast," "irrational animal." Such an expression as "We are only creatures" would almost certainly be misunderstood.

CRUCIFIXION, CROSS, etc. Centuries of hymnody and religious cant have so exhausted these words that they now very faintly—if at all—convey the idea of execution by torture. It is better to paraphrase; and, for the same reason, to say *flogged* for New Testament *scourged*.[12]

DOGMA. Used by the people only in a bad sense to mean "unproved assertion delivered in an arrogant manner."

IMMACULATE CONCEPTION. In the mouth of an uneducated speaker *always* means *Virgin Birth*.

MORALITY means *chastity*.

PERSONAL. I had argued for at least ten minutes with a man about the existence of a "personal devil" before I discovered that *personal* meant to him *corporeal*. I suspect this of being widespread. When they say they don't believe in a "personal" God they may often mean only that they are not anthropomorphists.

POTENTIAL. When used at all is used in an engineering sense: *never* means "possible."

[11]A phrase which occurs in the prayer of "Thanksgiving" at the end of the service of Holy Communion.
[12]Matthew xxvii. 26; Mark xv. 15; John xix. 1.

PRIMITIVE. Means crude, clumsy, unfinished, inefficient. "Primitive Christianity" would not mean to them at all what it does to you.

SACRIFICE. Has no associations with temple and altar. They are familiar with this word only in the journalistic sense ("The nation must be prepared for heavy sacrifices.").

SPIRITUAL. Means primarily *immaterial, incorporeal,* but with serious confusions from the Christians uses of πνεῦμα.[13] Hence the idea that whatever is "spiritual" in the sense of "nonsensuous" is somehow *better* than anything sensuous: e.g., they don't really believe that envy could be as bad as drunkenness.

VULGARITY. Usually means obscenity or "smut." There are bad confusions (and not only in uneducated minds) between: (a) The obscene or lascivious: what is calculated to provoke lust. (b) The indecorous: what offends against good taste or propriety. (c) The vulgar proper: what is socially "low." "Good" people tend to think (b) as sinful as (a) with the result that others feel (a) to be just as innocent as (b).

To conclude—you must translate every bit of your theology into the vernacular. This is very troublesome and it means you can say very little in half an hour, but it is essential. It is also of the greatest service to your own thought. I have come to the conviction that if you cannot translate your thoughts into uneducated language, then your thoughts were confused. Power to translate is the test of having really understood one's own meaning. A passage from some theological work for translation into the vernacular ought to be a compulsory paper in every ordination examination.

I turn now to the question of the actual attack. This may be either emotional or intellectual. If I speak only of the intellectual kind, that is not because I undervalue the other but because, not having been given the gifts necessary for carrying it out, I cannot give advice about it. But I wish to say most emphatically that where a speaker has that gift, the direct evangelical appeal of the "Come to Jesus" type can be as overwhelming today as it was a hundred years ago. I have seen it done, preluded by a religious film and accompanied by hymn singing,

---

[13]Which means "spirit," as in I Corinthians xiv. 12.

and with very remarkable effect. I cannot do it: but those who can ought to do it with all their might. I am not sure that the ideal missionary team ought not to consist of one who argues and one who (in the fullest sense of the word) preaches. Put up your arguer first to undermine their intellectual prejudices; then let the evangelist proper launch his appeal. I have seen this done with great success. But here I must concern myself only with the intellectual attack. *Non omnia possumus omnes.*[14]

And first, a word of encouragement. Uneducated people are not irrational people. I have found that they will endure, and can follow, quite a lot of sustained argument if you go slowly. Often, indeed, the novelty of it (for they have seldom met it before) delights them.

Do not attempt to water Christianity down. There must be no pretense that you can have it with the supernatural left out. So far as I can see, Christianity is precisely the one religion from which the miraculous cannot be separated. You must frankly argue for supernaturalism from the very outset.

The two popular "difficulties" you will probably have to deal with are these. (1) "Now that we know how huge the universe is and how insignificant the earth, it is ridiculous to believe that the universal God should be specially interested in our concerns." In answer to this you must first correct their error about *fact*. The insignificance of earth in relation to the universe is not a modern discovery: nearly two thousand years ago Ptolemy (*Almagest,* bk. 1, ch. v) said that in relation to the distance of the fixed stars earth must be treated as a mathematical point without magnitude. Secondly, you should point out that Christianity says what God has done for man; it doesn't say (because it doesn't know) what He has or has not done in other parts of the universe. Thirdly, you might recall the parable of the one lost sheep.[15] If earth has been specially sought by God (which we don't know) that may not imply that it is the most important thing in the universe, but only that it has *strayed*. Finally, challenge the whole tendency to identify size and importance. Is an elephant more important than a man, or a man's leg than his brain?

(2) "People believed in miracles in the old days because they didn't then know that they were contrary to the Laws of Nature." But they did. If St. Joseph didn't know that a virgin

[14]"Not all things can we all do," Virgil, *Eclogues,* bk. VIII, line 63.
[15]Matthew xviii. 11–14; Luke xv. 4–7.

birth was contrary to Nature (i.e. if he didn't know the normal origin of babies), why, on discovering his wife's pregnancy, was he "minded to put her away"?[16] Obviously, no event would be recorded as a wonder *unless* the recorders knew the natural order and saw that this was an exception. If people didn't yet know that the sun rose in the east, they wouldn't be even interested in its once rising in the west. They would not record it as a *miraculum*—nor indeed record it at all. The very idea of "miracle" presupposes knowledge of the Laws of Nature; you can't have the idea of an exception until you have the idea of a rule.

It is very difficult to produce arguments on the popular level for the existence of God. And many of the most popular arguments seem to me invalid. Some of these may be produced in discussion by friendly members of the audience. This raises the whole problem of the "embarrassing supporter." It is brutal (and dangerous) to repel him; it is often dishonest to agree with what he says. I usually try to avoid saying anything about the validity of his argument *in itself* and reply. "Yes. That may do for you and me. But I'm afraid if we take that line our friend here on my left might say etc. etc."

Fortunately, though very oddly, I have found that people are usually disposed to hear the divinity of our Lord discussed *before* going into the existence of God. When I began I used, if I were giving two lectures, to devote the first to mere theism; but I soon gave up this method because it seemed to arouse little interest. The number of clear and determined atheists is apparently not very large.

When we come to the Incarnation itself, I usually find that some form of the *aut Deus aut malus homo*[17] can be used. The majority of them start with the idea of the "great human teacher" who was deified by His superstitious followers. It must be pointed out how very improbable this is among Jews and how different to anything that happened with Plato, Confucius, Buddha, Mohammed. The Lord's own words and claims (of which many are quite ignorant) must be forced home. (The whole case, on a popular level, is very well put indeed in Chesterton's *The Everlasting Man.*)

Something will usually have to be said about the historicity of the Gospels. You who are trained theologians will be able

[16]Matthew i. 19.
[17]"Either God or a bad man."

to do this in ways which I could not. My own line was to say that I was a professional literary critic and I thought I did know the difference between legend and historical writing: that the Gospels were certainly not legends (in one sense they're not *good* enough): and that if they are not history, then they are realistic prose fiction of a kind which actually never existed before the eighteenth century. Little episodes such as Jesus writing in the dust when they brought Him the woman taken in adultery[18] (which have no *doctrinal* significance at all) are the mark.

One of the great difficulties is to keep before the audience's mind the question of truth. They always think you are recommending Christianity not because it is *true* but because it is *good*. And in the discussion they will at every moment try to escape from the issue "true—or false" into stuff about a good society, or morals, or the incomes of bishops, or the Spanish Inquisition, or France, or Poland—or anything whatever. You have to keep forcing them back, and again back, to the real point. Only thus will you be able to undermine (a) Their belief that a certain amount of "religion" is desirable but one mustn't carry it too far. One must keep on pointing out that Christianity is a statement which, if false, is of *no* importance, and if true, of infinite importance. The one thing it cannot be is moderately important. (b) Their firm disbelief of Article XVIII.[19] Of course it should be pointed out that, though all salvation is through Jesus, we need not conclude that He cannot save those who have not explicitly accepted Him in this life. And it should (at least in my judgement) be made clear that we are not pronouncing all other religions to be totally false, but rather saying that in Christ whatever is true in all religions is consummated and perfected. But, on the other hand, I think we must attack wherever we meet it the nonsensical idea that mutually exclusive propositions about God can both be true.

For my own part, I have sometimes told my audience that the only two things really worth considering are Christianity

[18]John viii. 3–8.

[19]Article XVIII in the Prayer Book: *Of obtaining eternal Salvation only by the Name of Christ*, which says "They also are to be had accursed that presume to say, That every man shall be saved by the Law or Sect which he professeth, so that he be diligent to frame his life according to that Law, and the light of Nature. For holy Scripture doth set out unto us only the Name of Jesus Christ, whereby men must be saved."

and Hinduism. (Islam is only the greatest of the Christian heresies, Buddhism only the greatest of the Hindu heresies. Real paganism is dead. All that was best in Judaism and Platonism survives in Christianity.) There isn't really, for an adult mind, this infinte variety of religions to consider. We may *salva reverentia*[20] divide religions, as we do soups, into "thick" and "clear." By *thick* I mean those which have orgies and ecstasies and mysteries and local attachments: Africa is full of thick religions. By *clear* I mean those which are philosophical, ethical, and universalizing: Stoicism, Buddhism, and the Ethical Church are clear religions. Now if there is a true religion, it must be both thick and clear: for the true God must have made both the child and the man, both the savage and the citizen, both the head and the belly. And the only two religions that fulfill this condition are Hinduism and Christianity. But Hinduism fulfills it imperfectly. The clear religion of the Brahman hermit in the jungle and the thick religion of the neighboring temple go on *side by side*. The Brahman hermit doesn't bother about the temple prostitution nor the worshiper in the temple about the hermit's metaphysics. But Christianity really breaks down the middle wall of the partition. It takes a convert from Central Africa and tells him to obey an enlightened universalist ethic: it takes a twentieth-century academic prig like me and tells me to go fasting to a mystery, to drink the blood of the Lord. The savage convert has to be clear: I have to be thick. That is how one knows one has come to the real religion.

One last word. I have found that nothing is more dangerous to one's own faith than the work of an apologist. No doctrine of that faith seems to me so spectral, so unreal as one that I have just successfully defended in a public debate. For a moment, you see, it has seemed to rest on oneself: as a result, when you go away from that debate, it seems no stronger than that weak pillar. That is why we apologists take our lives in our hands and can be saved only by falling back continually from the web of our own arguments, as from our intellectual counters, into the reality—from Christian apologetics into Christ Himself. That also is why we need one another's continual help—*oremus pro invicem*.[21]

---

[20]"Without outraging reverence."
[21]"Let us pray for each other."

10.

WORK AND PRAYER

Even if I grant your point and admit that answers to prayer are theoretically possible, I shall still think they are infinitely improbable. I don't think it at all likely that God requires the ill-informed (and contradictory) advice of us humans as to how to run the world. If He is all-wise, as you say He is, doesn't He know already what is best? And if He is all-good won't He do it whether we pray or not?"

This is the case against prayer which has, in the last hundred years, intimidated thousands of people. The usual answer is that it applies only to the lowest sort of prayer, the sort that consists in asking for things to happen. The higher sort, we are told, offers no advice to God; it consists only of "communion" or intercourse with Him; and those who take this line seem to suggest that the lower kind of prayer really is an absurdity and that only children or savages would use it.

I have never been satisfied with this view. The distinction between the two sorts of prayer is a sound one; and I think on the whole (I am not quite certain) that the sort which asks for nothing is the higher or more advanced. To be in the state in which you are so at one with the will of God that you wouldn't want to alter the course of events even if you could is certainly a very high or advanced condition.

But if one simply rules out the lower kind, two difficulties follow. In the first place, one has to say that the whole historical tradition of Christian prayer (including the Lord's Prayer itself) has always admitted prayers for our daily bread, for the recovery of the sick, for protection from enemies, for the conversion of the outside world, and the like. In the second place, though the other kind of prayer may be "higher," if you restrict yourself to it because you have got beyond the desire to use any other, there is nothing specially "high" or

77

"spiritual" about abstaining from prayers that make requests simply because you think they're no good. It might be a very pretty thing (but, again, I'm not absolutely certain) if a little boy never asked for cake because he was so high-minded and spiritual that he didn't want any cake. But there's nothing specially pretty about a little boy who doesn't ask because he has learned that it is no use asking. I think that the whole matter needs reconsideration.

The case against prayer (I mean the "low" or old-fashioned kind) is this. The thing you ask for is either good—for you and for the world in general—or else it is not. If it is, then a good and wise God will do it anyway. If it is not, then He won't. In neither case can your prayer make any difference. But if this argument is sound, surely it is an argument not only against praying, but against doing anything whatever?

In every action, just as in every prayer, you are trying to bring about a certain result; and this result must be good or bad. Why, then, do we not argue as the opponents of prayer argue, and say that if the intended result is good, God will bring it to pass without your interference, and that if it is bad, He will prevent it happening whatever you do? Why wash your hands? If God intends them to be clean, they'll come clean without your washing them. If He doesn't, they'll remain dirty (as Lady Macbeth found)[1] however much soap you use. Why ask for the salt? Why put on your boots? Why do anything?

We know that we can act and that our actions produce results. Everyone who believes in God must therefore admit (quite apart from the question of prayer) that God has not chosen to write the whole of history with His own hand. Most of the events that go on in the universe are indeed out of our control, but not all. It is like a play in which the scene and the general outline of the story is fixed by the author, but certain minor details are left for the actors to improvise. It may be a mystery why He should have allowed us to cause real events at all; but it is no odder that He should allow us to cause them by praying than by any other method.

Pascal says that God "instituted prayer in order to allow His creatures the dignity of causality." It would perhaps be truer to say that He invented both prayer and physical action for that purpose. He gave us small creatures the dignity of being able to contribute to the course of events in two different ways. He

[1]Shakespeare, *Macbeth*, V, i, 34–57.

made the matter of the universe such that we can (in those limits) do things to it; that is why we can wash our own hands and feed or murder our fellow creatures. Similarly, He made His own plan or plot of history such that it admits a certain amount of free play and can be modified in response to our prayers. If it is foolish and impudent to ask for victory in a war (on the ground that God might be expected to know best), it would be equally foolish and impudent to put on a mackintosh—does not God know best whether you ought to be wet or dry?

The two methods by which we are allowed to produce events may be called work and prayer. Both are alike in this respect—that in both we try to produce a state of affairs which God has not (or at any rate not yet) seen fit to provide "on His own." And from this point of view the old maxim *laborare est orare* (work is prayer) takes on a new meaning. What we do when we weed a field is not quite different from what we do when we pray for a good harvest. But there is an important difference all the same.

You cannot be sure of a good harvest whatever you do to a field. But you can be sure that if you pull up one weed that one weed will no longer be there. You can be sure that if you drink more than a certain amount of alcohol you will ruin your health or that if you go on for a few centuries more wasting the resources of the planet on wars and luxuries you will shorten the life of the whole human race. The kind of causality we exercise by work is, so to speak, divinely guaranteed, and therefore ruthless. By it we are free to do ourselves as much harm as we please. But the kind which we exercise by prayer is not like that; God has left Himself a discretionary power. Had He not done so, prayer would be an activity too dangerous for man and we should have the horrible state of things envisaged by Juvenal: "Enormous prayers which Heaven in anger grants."[2]

Prayers are not always—in the crude, factual sense of the word—"granted." This is not because prayer is a weaker kind of causality, but because it is a stronger kind. When it "works" at all it works unlimited by space and time. That is why God has retained a discretionary power of granting or refusing it; except on that condition prayer would destroy us. It is not unreasonable for a headmaster to say, "Such and such things

[2]*Satires*, Bk. IV, Satire x, line 111.

you may do according to the fixed rules of this school. But such and such other things are too dangerous to be left to general rules. If you want to do them you must come and make a request and talk over the whole matter with me in my study. And then—we'll see."

11.

MAN OR RABBIT?

"Can't you lead a good life without believing in Christianity?" This is the question on which I have been asked to write, and straight away, before I begin trying to answer it, I have a comment to make. The question sounds as if it were asked by a person who said to himself, "I don't care whether Christianity is in fact true or not. I'm not interested in finding out whether the real universe is more like what the Christians say than what the materialists say. All I'm interested in is leading a good life. I'm going to choose beliefs not because I think them true but because I find them helpful." Now frankly, I find it hard to sympathize with this state of mind. One of the things that distinguishes man from the other animals is that he wants to know things, wants to find out what reality is like, simply for the sake of knowing. When that desire is completely quenched in anyone, I think he has become something less than human. As a matter of fact, I don't believe any of you have really lost that desire. More probably, foolish preachers, by always telling you how much Christianity will help you and how good it is for society, have actually led you to forget that Christianity is not a patent medicine. Christianity claims to give an account of *facts*—to tell you what the real universe is like. Its account of the universe may be true, or it may not, and once the question is really before you, then your natural inquisitiveness must make you want to know the answer. If Christianity is untrue, then no honest man will want to believe it, however helpful it might be: if it is true, every honest man will want to believe it, even if it gives him no help at all.

As soon as we have realized this, we realize something else. If Christianity should happen to be true, then it is quite impossible that those who know this truth and those who don't should be equally well equipped for leading a good life. Knowledge of the facts must make a difference to one's actions. Suppose you found a man on the point of starvation and wanted to do the right thing. If you had no knowledge of medical science, you would probably give him a large solid meal; and as a result your man would die. That is what comes of working in the dark. In the same way a Christian and a non-Christian may both wish to do good to their fellow men. The one believes that men are going to live forever, that they were created by God and so built that they can find their true and lasting happiness only by being united to God, that they have gone badly off the rails, and that obedient faith in Christ is the only way back. The other believes that men are an accidental result of the blind workings of matter, that they started as mere animals and have more or less steadily improved, that they are going to live for about seventy years, that their happiness is fully attainable by good social services and political organizations, and that everything else (e.g., vivisection, birth control, the judicial system, education) is to be judged to be "good" or "bad" simply insofar as it helps or hinders that kind of "happiness."

Now there are quite a lot of things which these two men could agree in doing for their fellow citizens. Both would approve of efficient sewers and hospitals and a healthy diet. But sooner or later the difference of their beliefs would produce differences in their practical proposals. Both, for example, might be very keen about education: but the kinds of education they wanted people to have would obviously be very different. Again, where the materialist would simply ask about a proposed action, "Will it increase the happiness of the majority?" the Christian might have to say, "Even if it does increase the happiness of the majority, we can't do it. It is unjust." And all the time, one great difference would run through their whole policy. To the materialist things like nations, classes, civilizations must be more important than individuals, because the individuals live only seventy-odd years each and the group may last for centuries. But to the Christian, individuals are more important, for they live eternally; and races, civilizations and the like, are in comparison the creatures of a day.

The Christian and the materialist hold different beliefs about the universe. They can't both be right. The one who is wrong will act in a way which simply doesn't fit the real universe. Consequently, with the best will in the world, he will be helping his fellow creatures to their destruction.

With the best will in the world . . . then it won't be his fault. Surely God (if there is a God) will not punish a man for honest mistakes? But was *that* all you were thinking about? Are we ready to run the risk of working in the dark all our lives and doing infinite harm, provided only someone will assure us that our own skins will be safe, that no one will punish us or blame us? I will not believe that the reader is quite on that level. But even if he were, there is something to be said to him.

The question before each of us is not, "Can *someone* lead a good life without Christianity?" The question is, "Can *I?*" We all know there have been good men who were not Christians; men like Socrates and Confucius who had never heard of it, or men like J. S.Mill who quite honestly couldn't believe it. Supposing Christianity to be true, these men were in a state of honest ignorance or honest error. If their intentions were as good as I suppose them to have been (for of course I can't read their secret hearts), I hope and believe that the skill and mercy of God will remedy the evils which their ignorance, left to itself, would naturally produce both for them and for those whom they influenced. But the man who asks me, "Can't I lead a good life without believing in Christianity?" is clearly not in the same position. If he hadn't heard of Christianity he would not be asking this question. If, having heard of it, and having seriously considered it, he had decided that it was untrue, then once more he would not be asking the question. The man who asks this question has heard of Christianity and is by no means certain that it may not be true. He is really asking, "Need I bother about it? Mayn't I just evade the issue, just let sleeping dogs lie, and get on with being 'good'? Aren't good intentions enough to keep me safe and blameless without knocking at that dreadful door and making sure whether there is, or isn't someone inside?"

To such a man it might be enough to reply that he is really asking to be allowed to get on with being "good" before he has done his best to discover what *good* means. But that is not the whole story. We need not inquire whether God will punish him for his cowardice and laziness; they will punish themselves. The man is shirking. He is deliberately trying not to know whether Christianity is true or false, because he foresees endless trouble if it should turn out to be true. He is like the man who deliberately "forgets" to look at the notice board because, if he did, he might find his name down for some unpleasant duty. He is like the man who won't look at his bank account because he's afraid of what he might find there. He is like the man who won't go to the doctor when he first feels a mysterious pain, because he is afraid of what the doctor may tell him.

The man who remains an unbeliever for such reasons is not in a state of honest error. He is in a state of dishonest error, and that dishonesty will spread through all his thoughts and actions: a certain shiftiness, a vague worry in the background, a blunting of his whole mental edge, will result. He has lost his intellectual virginity. Honest rejection of Christ, however mistaken, will be forgiven and healed—"Whosoever shall speak a word against the Son of man, it shall be forgiven him."[1] But to *evade* the Son of man, to look the other way, to pretend you haven't noticed, to become suddenly absorbed in something on the other side of the street, to leave the receiver off the telephone because it might be He who was ringing up, to leave unopened certain letters in a strange handwriting because they might be from Him—this is a different matter. You may not be certain yet whether you ought to be a Christian; but you do know you ought to be a man, not an ostrich, hiding its head in the sand.

But still—for intellectual honor has sunk very low in our age—I hear someone whimpering on with his question, "Will it help me? Will it make me happy? Do you really think I'd be better if I became a Christian?" Well, if you must have it, my answer is "Yes." But I don't like giving an answer at all at this stage. Here is a door, behind which, according to some people, the secret of the universe is waiting for you. Either that's true, or it isn't. And if it isn't, then what the door really conceals is simply the greatest fraud, the most colossal "sell" on record. Isn't it obviously the job of every man (that is a man and not a rabbit) to try to find out which, and then to devote his full energies either to serving this tremendous secret or to exposing and destroying this gigantic humbug? Faced with such an issue, can you really remain wholly absorbed in your own blessed "moral development"?

All right, Christianity will do you good—a great deal more good than you ever wanted or expected. And the first bit of good it will do you is to hammer into your head (you won't enjoy *that*! the fact that what you have hitherto called "good"— all that about "leading a decent life" and "being kind"—isn't quite the magnificent and all-important affair you supposed. It will teach you that in fact you can't be "good" (not for twenty-four hours) on your own moral efforts. And then it will teach

[1] Luke xii. 10.

you that even if you were, you still wouldn't have achieved the purpose for which you were created. Mere *morality* is not the end of life. You were made for something quite different from that. J. S. Mill and Confucius (Socrates was much nearer the reality) simply didn't know what life is about. The people who keep on asking if they can't lead a decent life without Christ, don't know what life is about; if they did they would know that "a decent life" is mere machinery compared with the thing we men are really made for. Morality is indispensable: but the Divine Life, which gives itself to us and which calls us to be gods, intends for us something in which morality will be swallowed up. We are to be remade. All the rabbit in us is to disappear—the worried, conscientious, ethical rabbit as well as the cowardly and sensual rabbit. We shall bleed and squeal as the handfuls of fur come out; and then, surprisingly, we shall find underneath it all a thing we have never yet imagined: a real man, an ageless god, a son of God, strong, radiant, wise, beautiful, and drenched in joy.

"When that which is perfect is come, then that which is in part shall be done away."[2] The idea of reaching "a good life" without Christ is based on a double error. Firstly, we cannot do it; and secondly, in setting up "a good life" as our final goal, we have missed the very point of our existence. Morality is a mountain which we cannot climb by our own efforts; and if we could we should only perish in the ice and unbreathable air of the summit, lacking those wings with which the rest of the journey has to be accomplished. For it is *from* there that the real ascent begins. The ropes and axes are "done away" and the rest is a matter of flying.

[2] I Cor. xiii. 10.

12.

RELIGION WITHOUT DOGMA?[1]

Iɴ ʜɪs ᴘᴀᴘᴇʀ ᴏɴ "Tʜᴇ Gʀᴏᴜɴᴅs ᴏғ Mᴏᴅᴇʀɴ Aɢɴᴏsᴛɪᴄɪsᴍ," Professor Price maintains the following positions: (1) that the essence of religion is belief in God and immortality; (2) that in most actual religions the essence is found in connection with "accretions of dogma and mythology"[2] which have been rendered incredible by the progress of science; (3) that it would be very desirable, if it were possible, to retain the essence purged of the accretions; but (4) that science has rendered the essence almost as hard to believe as the accretions. For the doctrine of immortality involves the dualistic view that man is a composite creature, a soul in a state of symbiosis with a physical organism. But insofar as science can successfully regard man monistically, as a single organism whose psychological properties all arise from his physical, the soul becomes an indefensible hypothesis. In conclusion, Professor Price found our only hope in certain empirical evidence for the soul which

[1]This paper was originally read to the Oxford Socratic Club on May 20, 1946, as "Religion without Dogma?"; and later published in the *Phoenix Quarterly*, vol. I, No. 1 (Autumn 1946) under the title "A Christian Reply to Professor Price." It is an answer to "The Grounds of Modern Agnosticism," a paper which Professor Price read to the Socratic Club on October 23, 1944, and which was published in the same issue of the *Phoenix Quarterly*. Though Lewis's paper was afterwards reprinted in *The Socratic Digest* [1948], it is obvious from the fact that many errors which appear in the *Socratic* version were corrected in the *Quarterly* version, that the *Quarterly* version represents Lewis's final revision. I have incorporated in the text given here all the marginal emendations which Lewis made in his copy of the *Phoenix Quarterly*, as well as those portions from the *Socratic* version which he had omitted in his revision.

[2]H. H. Price, "The Grounds of Modern Agnosticism," *Phoenix Quarterly*, vol. I. No. 1 (Autumn 1946), p. 25.

appears to him satisfactory; in fact, in the findings of psychical research.

My disagreement with Professor Price begins, I am afraid, at the threshold. I do not define the essence of religion as belief in God and immortality. Judaism in its earlier stages had no belief in immortality, and for a long time no belief which was religiously relevant. The shadowy existence of the ghost in Sheol was one of which Jehovah took no account and which took no account of Jehovah. In Sheol all things are forgotten. The religion was centered on the ritual and ethical demands of Jehovah in the present life, and also, of course, on benefits expected from Him. These benefits are often merely worldly benefits (grandchildren and peace upon Israel), but a more specifically religious note is repeatedly struck. The Jew is athirst for the living God,[3] he delights in His laws as in honey or treasure,[4] he is conscious of himself in Jehovah's presence as unclean of lips and heart.[5] The glory or splendor of God is worshiped for its own sake. In Buddhism, on the other hand, we find that a doctrine of immortality is central, while there is nothing specifically religious. Salvation from immortality, deliverance from reincarnation, is the very core of its message. The existence of the gods is not necessarily decried, but it is of no religious significance. In Stoicism again both the religious quality and the belief in immortality are variables, but they do not vary in direct ratio. Even within Christianity itself we find a striking expression, not without influence from Stoicism, of the subordinate position of immortality. When Henry More ends a poem on the spiritual life by saying that if, after all, he should turn out to be mortal he would be

> . . . satisfide
> A lonesome mortall God t' have died.[6]

From my own point of view, the example of Judaism and Buddhism is of immense importance. The system, which is meaningless without a doctrine of immortality, regards im-

[3]Psalm xlii. 2.

[4]Psalm xix. 10.

[5]Isaiah vi. 5.

[6]"Resolution," *The Complete Poems of Dr. Henry More*, ed. Alexander B. Grosart (Edinburgh, 1878), line 117, p. 176.

mortality as a nightmare, not as a prize. The religion which, of all ancient religions, is most specifically religious, that is, at once most ethical and most numinous, is hardly interested in the question. Believing, as I do, that Jehovah is a real being, indeed the *ens realissimum*, I cannot sufficiently admire the divine tact of thus training the chosen race for centuries in religion before even hinting the shining secret of eternal life. He behaves like the rich lover in a romance who woos the maiden on his own merits, disguised as a poor man, and only when he has won her reveals that he has a throne and palace to offer. For I cannot help thinking that any religion which begins with a thirst for immortality is damned, as a religion, from the outset. Until a certain spiritual level has been reached, the promise of immortality will always operate as a bribe which vitiates the whole religion and infinitely inflames those very self-regards which religion must cut down and uproot. For the essence of religion, in my view, is the thirst for an end higher than natural ends; the finite self's desire for, and acquiescence in, and self-rejection in favor of, an object wholly good and wholly good for it. That the self-rejection will turn out to be also a self-finding, that bread cast upon the waters will be found after many days, that to die is to live—these are sacred paradoxes of which the human race must not be told too soon.

Differing from Professor Price about the essence of religion, I naturally cannot, in a sense, discuss whether the essence as he defines it coexists with accretions of dogma and mythology. But I freely admit that the essence as I define it always coexists with other things; and that some of these other things even I would call mythology. But my list of things mythological would not coincide with his, and our views of mythology itself probably differ. A great many different views on it have, of course, been held. Myths have been accepted as literally true, then as allegorically true (by the Stoics), as confused history (by Euhemerus),[7] as priestly lies (by the philosophers of the enlightenment), as imitative agricultural ritual mistaken for propositions (in the days of Frazer).[8] If you start from a naturalistic philos-

[7] A Sicilian writer (c. 315 B.C.) who developed the theory that the ancient beliefs about the gods originated from the elaboration of traditions of actual historical persons.

[8] James George Frazer, *The Golden Bough: A Study in Magic and Religion* (London, 1922).

ophy, then something like the view of Euhemerus or the view of Frazer is likely to result. But I am not a naturalist. I believe that in the huge mass of mythology which has come down to us a good many different sources are mixed—true history, allegory, ritual, the human delight in storytelling, etc. But among these sources I include the supernatural, both diabolical and divine. We need here concern ourselves only with the latter. If my religion is erroneous, then occurrences of similar motifs in pagan stories are, of course, instances of the same, or a similar error. But if my religion is true, then these stories may well be a *preparatio evangelica,* a divine hinting in poetic and ritual form at the same central truth which was later focused and (so to speak) historicized in the Incarnation. To me, who first approached Christianity from a delighted interest in, and reverence for, the best pagan imagination, who loved Balder before Christ and Plato before St. Augustine, the anthropological argument against Christianity has never been formidable. On the contrary, I could not believe Christianity if I were forced to say that there were a thousand religions in the world of which 999 were pure nonsense and the thousandth (fortunately) true. My conversion, very largely, depended on recognizing Christianity as the completion, the actualization, the entelechy, of something that had never been wholly absent from the mind of man. And I still think that the agnostic argument from similarities between Christianity and paganism works only if you know the answer. If you start by knowing on other grounds that Christianity is false, then the pagan stories may be another nail in its coffin: just as if you started by knowing that there were no such things as crocodiles, then the various stories about dragons might help to confirm your disbelief. But if the truth or falsehood of Christianity is the very question you are discussing, then the argument from anthropology is surely a *petitio*.

There are, of course, many things in Christianity which I accept as fact and which Professor Price would regard as mythology. In a word, there are miracles. The contention is that science has proved that miracles cannot occur. According to Professor Price "a deity who intervened miraculously and suspended natural law could never be accepted by Science;"[9] whence he passes on to consider whether we cannot still believe in

[9]Price, *op. cit.,* p. 20.

theism without miracles. I am afraid I have not understood why the miracles could never be accepted by one who accepted science.

Professor Price bases his view on the nature of scientific method. He says that that method is based on two assumptions. The first is that all events are subject to laws, and he adds: "It does not matter for our purpose whether the laws are 'deterministic' or only 'statistical.' "[10] But I submit that it matters to the scientist's view of the miraculous. The notion that natural laws may be merely statistical results from the modern belief that the individual unit of matter obeys no laws. Statistics were introduced to explain why, despite the lawlessness of the individual unit, the behavior of gross bodies was regular. The explanation was that, by a principle well known to actuaries, the law of averages leveled out the individual eccentricities of the innumerable units contained in even the smallest gross body. But with this conception of the lawless units the whole impregnability of nineteenth-century naturalism has, as it seems to me, been abandoned. What is the use of saying that all events are subject to laws if you also say that every event which befalls the individual unit of matter is *not* subject to laws. Indeed, if we define Nature as the system of events in spacetime governed by interlocking laws, then the new physics has really admitted that something other than Nature exists. For if Nature means the interlocking system, then the behavior of the individual unit is outside Nature. We have admitted what may be called the subnatural. After that admission what confidence is left us that there may not be a supernatural as well? It may be true that the lawlessness of the little events fed into Nature from the subnatural is always ironed out by the law of averages. It does not follow that great events could not be fed into her by the supernatural: nor that they also would allow themselves to be ironed out.

The second assumption which Professor Price attributes to the scientific method is "that laws can only be discovered by the study of publicly observable regularities."[11] Of course they can. This does not seem to me to be an assumption so much as a self-evident proposition. But what is it to the purpose? If a miracle occurs it is by definition an interruption of regularity. To discover a regularity is by definition not to discover its

[10]*Ibid.*
[11]*Ibid.*

interruptions, even if they occur. You cannot discover a railway accident from studying Bradshaw:[12] only by being there when it happens or hearing about it afterwards from someone who was. You cannot discover extra half holidays by studying a school timetable: you must wait till they are announced. But surely this does not mean that a student of Bradshaw is logically forced to deny the possibility of railway accidents. This point of scientific method merely shows (what no one to my knowledge ever denied) that if miracles *did* occur, science, as science, could not prove, or disprove, their occurrence. What cannot be trusted to recur is not material for science: that is why history is not one of the sciences. You cannot find out what Napoleon did at the battle of Austerlitz by asking him to come and fight it again in a laboratory with the same combatants, the same *terrain*, the same weather, and in the same age. You have to go to the records. We have not, in fact, proved that science excludes miracles: we have only proved that the question of miracles, like innumerable other questions, excludes laboratory treatment.

If I thus hand over miracles from science to history (but not, of course, to historians who beg the question by beginning with materialistic assumptions) Professor Price thinks I shall not fare much better. Here I must speak with caution, for I do not profess to be a historian or a textual critic. I would refer you to Sir Arnold Lunn's book *The Third Day*.[13] If Sir Arnold is right, then the biblical criticism which began in the nineteenth century has already shot its bolt and most of its conclusions have been successfully disputed, though it will, like nineteenth-century materialism, long continue to dominate popular thought. What I can say with more certainty is that that *kind* of criticism—the kind which discovers that every old book was made by six anonymous authors well provided with scissors and paste and that every anecdote of the slightest interest is unhistorical, has already begun to die out in the studies I know best. The period of arbitrary scepticism about the canon and text of Shakespeare is now over: and it is reasonable to expect that this method will soon be used only on Christian documents and survive only in the *Thinkers Library* and the theological colleges.

[12]George Bradshaw (1801–1853), who founded *Bradshaw's Railway Guide* which was published from 1839 to 1961.

[13](London, 1945).

I find myself, therefore, compelled to disagree with Professor Price's second point. I do not think that science has shown, or by its nature, could ever show that the miraculous element in religion is erroneous. I am not speaking, of course, about the psychological effects of science on those who practice it or read its results. That the continued application of scientific methods breeds a temper of mind unfavorable to the miraculous, may well be the case, but even here there would seem to be some difference among the sciences. Certainly, if we think, not of the miraculous in particular, but of religion in general there is such a difference. Mathematicians, astronomers, and physicists are often religious, even mystical; biologists much less often; economists and psychologists very seldom indeed. It is as their subject matter comes nearer to man himself that their antireligious bias hardens.

And that brings me to Professor Price's fourth point—for I would rather postpone consideration of his third. His fourth point, it will be remembered, was that science had undermined not only what he regards as the mythological accretions of religion, but also what he regards as its essence. That essence is for him theism and immortality. Insofar as natural science can give a satisfactory account of man as a purely biological entity, it excludes the soul and therefore excludes immortality. That, no doubt, is why the scientists who are most, or most nearly, concerned with man himself are the most antireligious.

Now most assuredly if naturalism is right, then it is at this point, at the study of man himself, that it wins its final victory and overthrows all our hopes: not only our hope of immortality, but our hope of finding significance in our lives here and now. On the other hand, if naturalism is wrong, it will be here that it will reveal its fatal philosophical defect, and that is what I think it does.

On the fully naturalistic view all events are determined by laws. Our logical behavior, in other words our thoughts, and our ethical behavior, including our ideals as well as our acts of will, are governed by biochemical laws; these, in turn, by physical laws which are themselves actuarial statements about the lawless movements of matter. These units never intended to produce the regular universe we see: the law of averages (successor to Lucretius's *exiguum clinamen*)[14] has produced it out of the collision of these random variations in movement.

[14]"small inclination," *De Rerum Natura*, bk. II, line 292.

The physical universe never intended to produce organisms. The relevant chemicals on earth, and the sun's heat, thus juxtaposed, gave rise to this disquieting disease of matter: organization. Natural selection, operating on the minute differences between one organism and another, blundered into that sort of phosphorescence or mirage which we call consciousness—and that, in some cortexes beneath some skulls, at certain moments, still in obedience to physical laws, but to physical laws now filtered through laws of a more complicated kind, takes the form we call thought. Such, for instance, is the origin of this paper: such was the origin of Professor Price's paper. What we should speak of as his "thoughts" were merely the last link of a causal chain in which all the previous links were irrational. He spoke as he did because the matter of his brain was behaving in a certain way: and the whole history of the universe up to that moment had forced it to behave in that way. What we called his thought was essentially a phenomenon of the same sort as his other secretions—the form which the vast irrational process of nature was bound to take at a particular point of space and time.

Of course it did not feel like that to him or to us while it was going on. He appeared to himself to be studying the nature of things, to be in some way aware of realities, even supersensuous realities, outside his own head. But if strict naturalism is right, he was deluded: he was merely enjoying the conscious reflection of irrationally determined events in his own head. It appeared to him that his thoughts (as he called them) could have to outer realities that wholly immaterial relation which we call truth or falsehood: though, in fact, being but the shadow of cerebral events, it is not easy to see that they could have any relation to the outer world except causal relations. And when Professor Price defended scientists, speaking of their devotion to truth and their constant following of the best light they knew, it seemed to him that he was choosing an attitude in obedience to an ideal. He did not feel that he was merely suffering a reaction determined by ultimately amoral and irrational sources, and no more capable of rightness or wrongness than a hiccup or a sneeze.

It would have been impossible for Professor Price to have written, or us to have read, his paper with the slightest interest if he and we had consciously held the position of strict naturalism throughout. But we can go further. It would be impossible to accept naturalism itself if we really and consistently believed naturalism. For naturalism is a system of thought. But for naturalism all thoughts are mere events with irrational causes.

It is, to me at any rate, impossible to regard the thoughts which make up naturalism in that way and, at the same time, to regard them as a real insight into external reality. Bradley distinguished *idea-event* from *idea-making*,[15] but naturalism seems to me committed to regarding ideas simply as events. For meaning is a relation of a wholly new kind, as remote, as mysterious, as opaque to empirical study, as soul itself.

Perhaps this may be even more simply put in another way. Every particular thought (whether it is a judgment of fact or a judgment of value) is always and by all men discounted the moment they believe that it can be explained, without remainder, as the result of irrational causes. Whenever you know what the other man is saying is wholly due to his complexes or to a bit of bone pressing on his brain, you cease to attach any importance to it. But if naturalism were true, then all thoughts whatever would be wholly the result of irrational causes. Therefore, all thoughts would be equally worthless. Therefore, naturalism is worthless. If it is true, then we can know no truths. It cuts its own throat.

I remember once being shown a certain kind of knot which was such that if you added one extra complication to make assurance doubly sure you suddenly found that the whole thing had come undone in your hands and you had only a bit of string. It is like that with naturalism. It goes on claiming territory after territory: first the inorganic, then the lower organisms, then man's body, then his emotions. But when it takes the final step and we attempt a naturalistic account of thought itself, suddenly the whole thing unravels. The last fatal step has invalidated all the preceding ones: for they were all reasonings and reason itself has been discredited. We must, therefore, either give up thinking altogether or else begin over again from the ground floor.

There is no reason, at this point, to bring in either Christianity or spiritualism. We do not need them to refute naturalism. It refutes itself. Whatever else we may come to believe about the universe, at least we cannot believe naturalism. The validity of rational thought, accepted in an utterly nonnaturalistic, transcendental (if you will), supernatural sense, is the necessary presupposition of all other theorizing. There is simply no sense in beginning with a view of the universe and trying

[15]"Spoken and Written English," *The Collected Papers of Henry Bradley*, ed. Robert Bridges (Oxford, 1928), pp. 168-93.

to fit the claims of thought in at a later stage. By thinking at all we have claimed that our thoughts are more than mere natural events. All other propositions must be fitted in as best they can round that primary claim.

Holding that science has not refuted the miraculous element in religion, much less that naturalism, rigorously taken, can refute anything except itself, I do not, of course, share Professor Price's anxiety to find a religion which can do without what he calls mythology. What he suggests is simple theism, rendered credible by a belief in immortality which, in its turn, is guaranteed by psychical research. Professor Price is not, of course, arguing that immortality would of itself prove theism: it would merely remove an obstacle to theism. The positive source of theism he finds in religious experience.

At this point it is very important to decide which of two questions we are asking. We may be asking: (1) whether this purged minimal religion suggested by Professor Price is capable, as an historical, social, and psychological entity, of giving fresh heart to society, strenghtening the moral will, and producing all those other benefits which, it is claimed, the old religions have sometimes produced. On the other hand, we may be asking: (2) whether this minimal religion will be the true one; that is, whether it contains the only true propositions we can make about ultimate questions.

The first question is not a religious question but a sociological one. The religious mind as such, like the older sort of scientific mind as such, does not care a rap about socially useful propositions. Both are athirst for reality, for the utterly objective, for that which is what it is. The "open mind" of the scientist and the emptied and silenced mind of the mystic are both efforts to eliminate what is our own in order that the other may speak. And if, turning aside from the religious attitude, we speak for a moment as mere sociologists, we must admit that history does not encourage us to expect much invigorating power in a minimal religion. Attempts at such a minimal religion are not new—from Akhenaten[16] and Julian the Apostate[17] down to

---

[16]Akhenaten (Amenhotep IV), king of Egypt, who came to the throne about 1375 B.C. and introduced a new religion, in which the sun-god Ra (designated as "Aten") superseded Amon.

[17]Roman emperor A.D. 361–3, who was brought up compulsorily as a Christian, but who on attaining the throne proclaimed himself a pagan, and made a great effort to revive the worship of the old gods.

Lord Herbert of Cherbury[18] and the late H. G. Wells. But where are the saints, the consolations, the ecstasies? The greatest of such attempts was that simplification of Jewish and Christian traditions which we call Islam. But it retained many elements which Professor Price would regard as mythical and barbaric, and its culture is by no means one of the richest or most progressive.

Nor do I see how such a religion, if it became a vital force, would long be preserved in its freedom from dogma. Is its God to be conceived pantheistically, or after the Jewish, Platonic, Christian fashion? If we are to retain the minimal religion in all its purity, I suppose the right answer would be: "We don't know, and we must be content not to know." But that is the end of the minimal religion as a practical affair. For the question is of pressing practical importance. If the God of Professor Price's religion is an impersonal spirituality diffused through the whole universe, equally present, and present in the same mode, at all points of space and time, then He—or it—will certainly be conceived as being beyond good and evil, expressed equally in the brothel or the torture chamber and in the model factory or the university common room. If, on the other hand, He is a personal Being standing outside His creation, commanding this and prohibiting that, quite different consequences follow. The choice between these two views affects the choice between courses of action at every moment both in private and public life. Nor is this the only such question that arises. Does the minimal religion know whether its god stands in the same relation to all men, or is he related to some as he is not related to others? To be true to its undogmatic character it must again say: "Don't ask." But if that is the reply, then the minimal religion cannot exclude the Christian view that He was present in a special way in Jesus, nor the Nazi view that He is present in a special way in the German race, nor the Hindu view that He is specially present in the Brahman, nor the Central African view that He is specially present in the thighbone of a dead English Tommy.

All these difficulties are concealed from us as long as the

---

[18]Edward Herbert (1583–1648). He is known as the "Father of deism," for he maintained that among the "common notions" apprehended by instinct are the existence of God, the duty of worship and repentance, and future rewards and punishment. This "natural religion," he believed, had been vitiated by superstition and dogma.

minimal religion exists only on paper. But suppose it were somehow established all over what is left of the British Empire, and let us suppose that Professor Price has (most reluctantly and solely from a sense of duty) become its supreme head on earth. I predict that one of two things must happen: (1) In the first month of his reign he will find himself uttering his first dogmatic definition—he will find himself saying, for example: "No. God is not an amoral force diffused through the whole universe to whom suttee and temple prostitution are no more and no less acceptable than building hospitals and teaching children; he is a righteous creator, separate from his creation, who demands of you justice and mercy" or (2) Professor Price will not reply. In the second case is it not clear what will happen? Those who have come to his minimal religion from Christianity will conceive God in the Jewish, Platonic, Christian way; those who have come from Hinduism will conceive Him pantheistically; and the plain men who have come from nowhere will conceive Him as a righteous creator in their moments of self-indulgence. And the ex-Marxist will think He is specially present in the proletariat, and the ex-Nazi will think He is specially present in the German people. And they will hold world conferences at which they all speak the same language and reach the most edifying agreement: but they will all mean totally different things. The minimal religion in fact cannot, while it remains minimal, be acted on. As soon as you *do* anything you have assumed one of the dogmas. In practice it will not be a religion at all; it will be merely a new coloring given to all the different things people were doing already.

I submit it to Professor Price, with great respect, that when he spoke of mere theism, he was all the time unconsciously assuming a particular conception of God: that is, he was assuming a dogma about God. And I do not think he was deducing it solely, or chiefly from his own religious experience or even from a study of religious experience in general. For religious experience can be made to yield almost any sort of God. I think Professor Price assumed a certain sort of God because he has been brought up in a certain way: because Bishop Butler and Hooker and Thomas Aquinas and Augustine and St. Paul and Christ and Aristotle and Plato are, as we say, "in his blood." He was not really starting from scratch. Had he done so, had God meant in his mind a being about whom no dogma whatever is held, I doubt whether he would have looked for even social salvation in such an empty concept. All the strength and value of the minimal religion, for him as for all others who accept it, is derived not from it, but from the tradition which he imports into it.

The minimal religion will, in my opinion, leave us all doing what we were doing before. Now it, in itself, will not be an objection from Professor Price's point of view. He was not working for unity, but for some spiritual dynamism to see us through the black night of civilization. If psychical research has the effect of enabling people to continue, or to return to, all the diverse religions which naturalism has threatened, and if they can thus get power and hope and discipline, he will, I fancy, be content. But the trouble is that if this minimal religion leaves Buddhists still Buddhists, and Nazis still Nazis, then it will, I believe, leave us—as Western, mechanized, democratic, secularized men—exactly where we were. In what way will a belief in the immortality vouched for by psychical research, and in an unknown God, restore to us the virtue and energy of our ancestors? It seems to me that both beliefs, unless reinforced by something else, will be to modern man very shadowy and inoperative. If indeed we knew that God were righteous, that He had purposes for us, that He was the leader in a cosmic battle and that some real issue hung on our conduct in the field, then it would be something to the purpose. Or if, again, the utterances which purport to come from the other world ever had the accent which really *suggests* another world, ever spoke (as even the inferior actual religions do) with the voice before which our mortal nature trembles with awe or joy, then that also would be to the purpose. But the god of minimal theism remains powerless to excite either fear or love: can be given power to do so only from those traditional resources to which, in Professor Price's conception, science will never permit our return. As for the utterances of the mediums . . . I do not wish to be offensive. But will even the most convinced spiritualist claim that one sentence from that source has ever taken its place among the golden sayings of mankind, has ever approached (much less equaled) in power to elevate, strengthen or correct even the second rank of such sayings? Will anyone deny that the vast majority of spirit messages sink pitiably below the best that has been thought and said even in this world?—that in most of them we find a banality and provincialism, a paradoxical union of the prim with the enthusiastic, of flatness and gush, which would suggest that the souls of the moderately respectable are in the keeping of Annie Besant[19] and Martin Tupper?[20]

I am not arguing from the vulgarity of the messages that their claim to come from the dead is false. If I did the spiritualist would reply that this quality is due to imperfections in the medium of communication. Let it be so. We are not here discussing the truth of spiritualism, but its power to become the starting point of a religion. And for that purpose I submit that the poverty of its contents disqualifies it. A minimal religion compounded of spirit messages and bare theism has no power to touch any of the deepest chords in our nature, or to evoke any response which will raise us even to a higher secular level—let alone to the spiritual life. The god of whom no dogmas are believed is a mere shadow. He will not produce that fear of the Lord in which wisdom begins, and therefore, will not produce that love in which it is consummated. The immortality which the messages suggest can produce in mediocre spirits only a vague comfort for our unredeemedly personal hankerings, a shadowy sequel to the story of this world in which all comes right (but right in how pitiable a sense!), while the more spiritual will feel that it has added a new horror to death—the horror of mere endless succession, of indefinite imprisonment in that which binds us all, *das Gemeine*.[21] There is in this minimal religion nothing that can convince, convert, or (in the higher sense) console; nothing, therefore, which can restore vitality to our civilization. It is not costly enough. It can never be a controller or even a rival to our natural sloth and greed. A flag, a song, an old school tie, is stronger than it; much more, the pagan religions. Rather than pin my hopes on it I would almost listen again to the drumbeat in my blood (for the blood is at least in some sense the life) and join in the song of the Maenads:

> Happy they whom the Daimons
> Have befriended, who have entered

[19]Annie Besant (1847–1933) was an ardent supporter of liberal causes and became a member of the Theosophical Society in 1889.

[20]Martin Tupper (1810–89) is probably best known for his *Proverbial Philosophy*—commonplace maxims and reflections couched in a rhythmical form.

[21]Johann Wolfgang Goethe, *Epilog zu Schillers Glocke*, 1. 32. "*das Gemeine*" means something like "that which dominates us all."

>The divine orgies, making holy
>Their life-days, till the dance throbs
>In their heart-beats, while they romp with
>Dionysus on the mountains. . . .[22]

Yes, almost; almost I'd sooner be a pagan suckled in a creed outworn

Almost, but not, of course, quite. If one is forced to such an alternative, it is perhaps better to starve in a wholly secularized and meaningless universe than to recall the obscenities and cruelties of paganism. They attract because they are a distortion of the truth, and therefore, retain some of its flavor. But with this remark I have passed into our second question. I shall not be expected at the end of this paper to begin an apologetic for the truth of Christianity. I will only say something which in one form or another I have said perhaps too often already. If there is no God, then we have no interest in the minimal religion or any other. We will not make a lie even to save civilization. But if there is, then it is so probable as to be almost axiomatic that the initiative lies wholly on His side. If He can be known it will be by self-revelation on His part, not by speculation on ours. We, therefore, look for Him where it is claimed that He has revealed Himself by miracle, by inspired teachers, by enjoined ritual. The traditions conflict, yet the longer and more sympathetically we study them the more we become aware of a common element in many of them: the theme of sacrifice, of mystical communion through the shed blood, of death and rebirth, of redemption, is too clear to escape notice. We are fully entitled to use moral and intellectual criticism. What we are not, in my opinion, entitled to do is simply to abstract the ethical element and set that up as a religion on its own. Rather in that tradition which is at once more completely ethical and most transcends mere ethics—in which the old themes of the sacrifice and rebirth recur in a form which transcends, though there it no longer revolts, our conscience and our reason—we may still most reasonably believe that we have the consummation of all religion, the fullest message from the wholly other, the living creator, who, if He is at all, must be the God not only of the philosophers, but of mystics and savages, not only of the head and heart, but also of the primitive emotions and the spiritual heights beyond all emotion. We may still reasonably attach ourselves to the church, to the only

[22]Euripides, *Bacchae*, 1. 74.

concrete organization which has preserved down to this present time the core of all the messages, pagan and perhaps prepagan, that have ever come from beyond the world, and begin to practice the only religion which rests not upon some selection of certain supposedly "higher" elements in our nature, but on the shattering and rebuilding, the death and rebirth, of that nature in every part; neither Greek nor Jew nor barbarian, but a new creation.

[*NOTE:* The debate between Lewis and Professor Price did not end here. In *The Socratic Digest*, No. 4 [1948], there follows a "Reply" to Lewis's "Religion Without Dogma?" by Professor Price (pp. 94–102). Then, at a meeting of the Socratic Club on February 2, 1948, Miss G. E. M. Anscombe read a paper entitled "A Reply to Mr. C. S. Lewis's Argument that 'Naturalism is Self-Refuting,'" afterwards published in the same issue of the *Digest* (pp. 7–15) as Professor Price's "Reply." Miss Anscombe criticized the argument found on pp. 92–95 of the paper printed above as well as chapter III, "The Self-Contradiction of the Naturalist," of Lewis's book *Miracles* (London, 1947). The two short pieces that follow are (A) the Socratic minute-book account of Lewis's reply to Miss Anscombe and (B) a reply written by Lewis himself—both reprinted from the same issue of the *Digest* mentioned above (pp. 15–16). Aware that the third chapter of his *Miracles* was ambiguous, Lewis revised this chapter for the Fontana (1960) issue of *Miracles* in which chapter III is retitled "The Cardinal Difficulty of Naturalism."]

A

In his reply Mr. C. S. Lewis agreed that the words "cause" and "ground" were far from synonymous but said that the recognition of a ground could be the cause of assent, and that assent was only rational when such was its cause. He denied that such words as "recognition" and "perception" could be properly used of a mental act among whose causes the thing perceived or recognized was not one.

Miss Anscombe said that Mr. Lewis had misunderstood her and thus the first part of the discussion was confined to the two speakers who attempted to clarify their positions and their differences. Miss Anscombe said that Mr. Lewis was still not distinguishing between "having reasons" and "having reasoned" in the causal sense. Mr. Lewis understood the speaker to be making a tetrachotomy thus: (1) logical reasons; (2) having reasons (i.e. psychological); (3) historical causes; (4) scientific causes or observed regularities. The main point in his reply was that an observed regularity was only the symptom of a cause, and not the cause itself, and in reply to an interruption by the secretary he referred to his notion of cause as "magical." An open discussion followed, in which some members tried to show Miss Anscombe that there was a connection between ground and cause, while others contended against the president [Lewis] that the test for the validity of reason could never in any event be such a thing as the state of the bloodstream. The president finally admitted that the word "valid" was an unfortunate one. From the discussion in general it appeared that Mr. Lewis would have to turn his argument into a rigorous analytic one, if his notion of "validity" as the effect of causes were to stand the test of all the questions put to him.

B

I admit that *valid* was a bad word for what I meant; *verdical* (or *verific* or *veriferous*) would have been better. I also admit that the cause and effect relation between events and the ground and consequent relation between propositions are distinct. Since English uses the word *because* of both, let us here use *because* CE for the cause-and-effect relation ("This doll always falls on its feet *because* CE its feet are weighted") and *because* GC for the ground and consequent relation ("A equals C *because* GC they both equal B"). But the sharper this distinction becomes the more my difficulty increases. If an argument is to be verific the conclusion must be related to the premises as consequent to ground, i.e. the conclusion is there *because* GC certain other propositions are true. On the other hand, our thinking the conclusion is an event and must be related to previous events as effect to cause, i.e. this act of thinking must occur *because* CE previous events have occured. It would seem, therefore, that we never think the conclusion *because* GC it is the consequent of its grounds but only *because* CE certain previous events have happened. If so, it does not seem that the GC sequence makes us more likely to think the true conclusion than not. And this is very much what I meant by the difficulty in naturalism.

13.

SOME THOUGHTS

At FIRST SIGHT NOTHING SEEMS MORE OBVIOUS THAN THAT religious persons should care for the sick; no Christian building, except perhaps a church, is more self-explanatory than a Christian hospital. Yet on further consideration the thing is really connected with the undying paradox, the blessedly two-edged character, of Christianity. And if any of us were now encountering Christianity for the first time he would be vividly aware of this paradox.

Let us suppose that such a person began by observing those Christian activities which are, in a sense, directed toward this present world. He would find that this religion had, as a mere matter of historical fact, been the agent which preserved such secular civilization as survived the fall of the Roman Empire; that to it Europe owes the salvation, in those perilous ages, of civilized agriculture, architecture, laws, and literacy itself. He would find this same religion has always been healing the sick and caring for the poor; that it has, more than any other, blessed marriage; and that arts and philosophy tend to flourish in its neighborhood. In a word, it is always either doing, or at least repenting with shame for not having done, all the things which secular humanitarianism enjoins. If our inquirer stopped at this point he would have no difficulty in classifying Christianity— giving it its place on a map of the "great religions." Obviously (he would say), this is one of the world-affirming religions like Confucianism or the agricultural religions of the great Mesopotamian city-states.

But how if our inquirer began (as he well might) with quite a different series of Christian phenomena? He might notice that the central image in all Christian art was that of a Man slowly dying by torture; that the instrument of His torture was the worldwide symbol of the faith; that martyrdom was almost a specifically Christian action; that our calendar was as full of fasts as of feasts; that we meditated constantly on the mortality not only of ourselves but of the whole universe; that we were bidden to entrust all our treasure to another world; and that even a certain disdain for the whole natural order (*contemptus mundi*) had sometimes been reckoned a Christian virtue. And here, once again, if he knew no more, the inquirer would find Christianity quite easy to classify; but this time he would classify it as one of the world-denying religions. It would be pigeonholed along with Buddhism.

Either conclusion would be justified if a man had only the one or the other half of the evidence before him. It is when he puts both halves together and sees that Christianity cuts right across the classification he was attempting to make—it is then that he first knows what he is up against, and I think he will be bewildered.

Probably most of those who read this page have been Christians all their lives. If so, they may find it hard to sympathize with the bewilderment I refer to. To Christians the explanation of this two-edged character in their faith seems obvious. They live in a graded or hierarchical universe where there is a place for everything and everything should be kept in its right place. The supernatural is higher than the natural, but each has its place; just as a man is higher than a dog, but a dog has its place. It is, therefore, to us not at all surprising that healing for the sick and provision for the poor should be less important than (when they are, as sometimes happens, alternative to) the salvation of souls; and yet very important. Because God created the natural—invented it out of His love and artistry—it demands our reverence; because it is only a creature and not He, it is, from another point of view, of little account. And still more, because Nature, and especially human nature, is fallen it must be corrected and the evil within it must be mortified. But its essence is good; correction is something quite different from Manichaean repudiation or Stoic superiority. Hence, in all true Christian asceticism, that respect for the thing rejected which, I think, we never find in pagan asceticism. Marriage is good, though not for me; wine is good, though I must not drink it; feasts are good, though today we fast.

This attitude will, I think, be found to depend logically on the doctrines of the Creation and the Fall. Some hazy adumbrations of a doctrine of the Fall can be found in paganism; but it is quite astonishing how rarely outside Christianity we

find—I am not sure that we ever find—a real doctrine of
Creation. In polytheism the gods are usually the product of a
universe already in existence—Keats's *Hyperion*, in spirit, if
not in detail, is true enough as a picture of pagan theogony.
In pantheism the universe is never something that God made.
It is an emanation, something that oozes out of Him, or an
appearance, something He looks like to us but really is not, or
even an attack of incurable schizophrenia from which He is
unaccountably suffering. Polytheism is always, in the long run,
nature worship; pantheism always, in the long run, hostility to
Nature. None of these beliefs really leaves you free *both* to
enjoy your breakfast *and* to mortify your inordinate appetites—
much less to mortify appetites recognized as innocent at present
lest they should become inordinate.

And none of them leaves anyone free to do what is being
done in the Lourdes Hospital every day: to fight against death
as earnestly, skillfully, and calmly as if you were a secular
humanitarian while knowing all the time that death is, both for
better and worse, something that the secular humanitarian has
never dreamed of. The world, knowing how all our real in-
vestments are beyond the grave, might expect us to be less
concerned than other people who go in for what is called Higher
Thought and tell us that "death doesn't matter"; but we "are
not high minded,"[1] and we follow one who stood and wept at
the grave of Lazarus—not surely, because He was grieved that
Mary and Martha wept, and sorrowed for their lack of faith
(though some thus interpret) but because death, the punishment
of sin, is even more horrible in His eyes than in ours. The
nature which He had created as God, the nature which He had
assumed as man, lay there before Him in its ignominy; a foul
smell, food for worms. Though He was to revive it a moment
later, He wept at the shame; if I may here quote a writer of
my own communion, "I am not so much afraid of death as
ashamed of it."[2] And that brings us again to the paradox. Of
all men, we hope most of death; yet nothing will reconcile us
to—well, its *unnaturalness*. We know that we were not made
for it; we know how it crept into our destiny as an intruder;

[1]Psalm cxxxi. 1.

[2]The reference is to Sir Thomas Browne's *Religio Medici*, First Part,
Section 40, where he says "I am not so much afraid of death, as ashamed
thereof."

and we know who has defeated it. Because our Lord is risen we know that on one level it is an enemy already disarmed; but because we know that the natural level also is God's creation we cannot cease to fight against the death which mars it, as against all those other blemishes upon it, against pain and poverty, barbarism and ignorance. Because we love something else more than this world we love even this world better than those who know no other.

14.

"THE TROUBLE
WITH 'X'..."

I SUPPOSE I MAY ASSUME THAT SEVEN OUT OF TEN OF THOSE
who read these lines are in some kind of difficulty about some
other human being. Either at work or at home, either the people
who employ you or those whom you employ, either those who
share your house or those whose house you share, either your
in-laws or parents or children, your wife or your husband, are
making life harder for you than it need be even in these days.
It is to be hoped that we do not often mention these difficulties
(especially the domestic ones) to outsiders. But sometimes we
do. An outside friend asks us why we are looking so glum,
and the truth comes out.

On such occasions the outside friend usually says, "But why
don't you tell them? Why don't you go to your wife (or husband, or father, or daughter, or boss, or landlady, or lodger)
and have it all out? People are usually reasonable. All you've
got to do is to make them see things in the right light. Explain
it to them in a reasonable, quiet, friendly way." And we,
whatever we say outwardly, think sadly to ourselves, "He doesn't
know 'X.'" We do. We know how utterly hopeless it is to
make "X" see reason. Either we've tried it over and over again—
tried it till we are sick of trying it—or else we've never tried
it because we saw from the beginning how useless it would
be. We know that if we attempt to "have it all out with 'X'"
there will either be a "scene," or else "X" will stare at us in
blank amazement and say, "I don't know on what earth you're
talking about"; or else (which is perhaps worst of all) "X" will
quite agree with us and promise to turn over a new leaf and
put everything on a new footing—and then, twenty-four hours
later, will be exactly the same as "X" has always been.

You know, in fact, that any attempt to talk things over with
"X" will shipwreck on the old, fatal flaw in "X's" character.
And you see, looking back, how all the plans you have ever

made always have shipwrecked on that fatal flaw—on "X's" incurable jealousy, or laziness, or touchiness, or muddlehead-edness, or bossiness, or ill temper, or changeableness. Up to a certain age you have perhaps had the illusion that some external stroke of good fortune—an improvement in health, a rise of salary, the end of the war—would solve your difficulty. But you know better now. The war is over, and you realize that even if the other things happened, "X" would still be "X," and you would still be up against the same old problem. Even if you became a millionaire, your husband would still be a bully, or your wife would still nag or your son would still drink, or you'd still have to have your mother-in-law to live with you.

It is a great step forward to realize that this is so; to face the fact that even if all external things went right, real happiness would still depend on the character of the people you have to live with—and that you can't alter their characters. And now comes the point. When you have seen this you have, for the first time, had a glimpse of what it must be like for God. For, of course, this is (in one way) just what God Himself is up against. He has provided a rich, beautiful world for people to live in. He has given them intelligence to show them how it can be used, and conscience to show them how it ought to be used. He has contrived that the things they need for their bi-ological life (food, drink, rest, sleep, exercise) should be pos-itively delightful to them. And, having done all this, He then sees all His plans spoiled—just as our little plans are spoiled— by the crookedness of the people themselves. All the things He has given them to be happy with they turn into occasions for quarreling and jealousy, and excess and hoarding, and tom-foolery.

You may say it is very different for God because He could, if He pleased, alter people's characters, and we can't. But this difference doesn't go quite as deep as we may at first think. God has made it a rule for Himself that He won't alter people's character by force. He can and will alter them—but only if the people will let Him. In that way He has really and truly limited His power. Sometimes we wonder why He has done so, or even wish that He hadn't. But apparently He thinks it worth doing. He would rather have a world of free beings, with all its risks, than a world of people who did right like machines because they couldn't do anything else. The more we succeed in imagining what a world of perfect automatic beings would be like, the more, I think, we shall see His wisdom.

I said that when we see how all our plans shipwreck on the characters of the people we have to deal with, we are "in *one* way" seeing what it must be like for God. But only in one way. There are two respects in which God's view must be very different from ours. In the first place, He sees (like you) how all the people in your home or your job are in various degrees awkward or difficult; but when He looks into that home or factory or office He sees one more person of the same kind— the one you never do see. I mean, of course, yourself. That is the next great step in wisdom—to realize that you also are just that sort of person. You also have a fatal flaw in your character. All the hopes and plans of others have again and again ship- wrecked on your character just as your hopes and plans have shipwrecked on theirs.

It is no good passing this over with some vague, general admission such as "Of course, I know I have my faults." It is important to realize that there is some really fatal flaw in you: something which gives the others just that same feeling of *despair* which their flaws give you. And it is almost certainly something you don't know about—like what the advertise- ments call "halitosis," which everyone notices except the per- son who has it. But why, you ask, don't the others tell me? Believe me, they have tried to tell you over and over again, and you just couldn't "take it." Perhaps a good deal of what you call their "nagging" or "bad temper" or "queerness" are just their attempts to make you see the truth. And even the faults you do know you don't know fully. You say, "I admit I lost my temper last night"; but the others know that you're always doing it, that you are a bad-tempered person. You say, "I admit I drank too much last Saturday"; but every one else knows that you are an habitual drunkard.

That is one way in which God's view must differ from mine. He sees all the characters: I see all except my own. But the second difference is this. He loves the people in spite of their faults. He goes on loving. He does not let go. Don't say, "It's all very well for Him; He hasn't got to live with them." He has. He is inside them as well as outside them. He is *with* them far more intimately and closely and incessantly than we can ever be. Every vile thought within their minds (and ours), every moment of spite, envy, arrogance, greed, and self-conceit comes right up against His patient and longing love, and grieves His spirit more than it grieves ours.

The more we can imitate God in both these respects, the more progress we shall make. We must love "X" more; and we must learn to see ourselves as a person of exactly the same kind. Some people say it is morbid to be always thinking of one's own faults. That would be all very well if most of us could stop thinking of our own without soon beginning to think about those of other people. For unfortunately we *enjoy* thinking about other people's faults: and in the proper sense of the word "morbid," that is the most morbid pleasure in the world.

We don't like rationing which is imposed upon us, but I suggest one form of rationing which we ought to impose on ourselves. Abstain from all thinking about other people's faults, unless your duties as a teacher or parent make it necessary to think about them. Whenever the thoughts come unnecessarily into one's mind, why not simply shove them away? And think of one's own faults instead? For there, with God's help, one *can* do something. Of all the awkward people in your house or job there is only one whom you can improve very much. That is the practical end at which to begin. And really, we'd better. The job has to be tackled some day: and every day we put it off will make it harder to begin.

What, after all, is the alternative? You see clearly enough that nothing, not even God with all His power, can make "X" really happy as long as "X" remains envious, self-centered, and spiteful. Be sure there is something inside you which, unless it is altered, will put it out of God's power to prevent your being eternally miserable. While that something remains there can be no heaven for you, just as there can be no sweet smells for a man with a cold in the nose, and no music for a man who is deaf. It's not a question of God "sending" us to hell. In each of us there is something growing up which will of itself *be hell* unless it is nipped in the bud. The matter is serious: let us put ourselves in His hands at once—this very day, this hour.

15.

WHAT ARE WE TO MAKE OF JESUS CHRIST?

WHAT ARE WE TO MAKE OF JESUS CHRIST? THIS IS A question which has, in a sense, a frantically comic side. For the real question is not what are we to make of Christ, but what is He to make of us? The picture of a fly sitting deciding what it is going to make of an elephant has comic elements about it. But perhaps the questioner meant what are we to make of Him in the sense of "How are we to solve the historical problem set us by the recorded sayings and acts of this Man?" This problem is to reconcile two things. On the one hand you have got the almost generally admitted depth and sanity of His moral teaching, which is not very seriously questioned, even by those who are opposed to Christianity. In fact, I find when I am arguing with very anti-God people that they rather make a point of saying, "I am entirely in favor of the moral teaching of Christianity"—and there seems to be a general agreement that in the teaching of this Man and of His immediate followers, moral truth is exhibited at its purest and best. It is not sloppy idealism, it is full of wisdom and shrewdness. The whole thing is realistic, fresh to the highest degree, the product of a sane mind. That is one phenomenon.

The other phenomenon is the quite appalling nature of this Man's theological remarks. You all know what I mean, and I want rather to stress the point that the appalling claim which this Man seems to be making is not merely made at one moment of His career. There is, of course, the one moment which led to His execution. The moment at which the high priest said to Him, "Who are you?" "I am the Anointed, the Son of the uncreated God, and you shall see Me appearing at the end of all history as the judge of the Universe." But that claim, in fact, does not rest on this one dramatic moment. When you look into His conversation you will find this sort of claim running through the whole thing. For instance, He went about saying to people, "I forgive your sins." Now it is quite natural for a man to forgive something you do to *him*. Thus if somebody cheats *me* out of £5 it is quite possible and reasonable for me to say, "Well, I forgive him, we will say no more about it." What on earth would you say if somebody had done *you* out of £ 5 and *I* said, "That is all right, I forgive him"? Then there is a curious thing which seems to slip out almost by accident. On one occasion this Man is sitting looking down on Jerusalem from the hill above it and suddenly in comes an extraordinary remark—"I keep on sending you prophets and wise men." Nobody comments on it. And yet, quite suddenly, almost incidentally, He is claiming to be the power that all through the centuries is sending wise men and leaders into the world. Here is another curious remark: in almost every religion there are unpleasant observances like fasting. This Man suddenly remarks one day, "No one need fast while I am here." Who is this Man who remarks that His mere presence suspends all normal rules? Who is the person who can suddenly tell the school they can have a half holiday? Sometimes the statements put forward the assumption that He, the Speaker, is completely without sin or fault. This is always the attitude. "You, to whom I am talking, are all sinners," and He never remotely suggests that this same reproach can be brought against Him. He says again, "I am begotten of the One God, before Abraham was, I am," and remember what the words "I am" were in Hebrew. They were the name of God, which must not be spoken by any human being, the name which it was death to utter.

Well, that is the other side. On the one side clear, definite moral teaching. On the other, claims which, if not true, are those of a megalomaniac, compared with whom Hitler was the most sane and humble of men. There is no halfway house and there is no parallel in other religions. If you had gone to Buddha and asked him "Are you the son of Bramah?" he would have said, "My son, you are still in the vale of illusion." If you had gone to Socrates and asked, "Are you Zeus?" he would have laughed at you. If you had gone to Mohammed and asked, "Are you Allah?" he would first have rent his clothes and then cut your head off. If you had asked Confucius, "Are you Heaven?" I think he would have probably replied, "Remarks which are not in accordance with Nature are in bad taste." The idea of a great moral teacher saying what Christ said is out of the question. In my opinion, the only person who can say that sort of thing is either God or a complete lunatic suffering from that form of delusion which undermines the whole mind of man. If you think you are a poached egg, when you are looking for a piece of toast to suit you, you may be sane, but if you think you are God, there is no chance for you. We may note in passing that He was never regarded as a mere moral teacher. He did not produce that effect on any of the people who actually met Him. He produced mainly three effects—hatred—terror—adoration. There was no trace of people expressing mild approval.

What are we to do about reconciling the two contradictory phenomena? One attempt consists in saying that the Man did not really say these things, but that His followers exaggerated the story, and so the legend grew up that He had said them. This is difficult because His followers were all Jews; that is, they belonged to that nation which of all others was most convinced that there was only one God—that there could not possibly be another. It is very odd that this horrible invention about a religious leader should grow up among the one people in the whole earth least likely to make such a mistake. On the contrary we get the impression that none of His immediate followers or even of the New Testament writers embraced the doctrine at all easily.

Another point is that on that view you would have to regard the accounts of the Man as being *legends*. Now, as a literary historian, I am perfectly convinced that whatever else the Gospels are they are not legends. I have read a great deal of legend and I am quite clear that they are not the same sort of thing. They are not artistic enough to be legends. From an imaginative point of view they are clumsy, they don't work up to things properly. Most of the life of Jesus is totally unknown to us, as is the life of anyone else who lived at that time, and no people building up a legend would allow that to be so. Apart from bits of the Platonic dialogues, there are no conversations that I know of in ancient literature like the Fourth Gospel. There is nothing, even in modern literature, until about a hundred years ago when the realistic novel came into existence. In the story of the woman taken in adultery we are told Christ bent down and scribbled in the dust with His finger. Nothing comes of this. No one has ever based any doctrine on it. And the art of *inventing* little irrelevant details to make an imaginary scene more convincing is a purely modern art. Surely the only explanation of this passage is that the thing really happened? The author put it in simply because he had *seen* it.

Then we come to the strangest story of all, the story of the Resurrection. It is very necessary to get the story clear. I heard a man say, "The importance of the Resurrection is that it gives evidence of survival, evidence that the human personality survives death." On that view what happened to Christ would be what had always happened to all men, the difference being that in Christ's case we were privileged to see it happening. This is certainly not what the earliest Christian writers thought. Something perfectly new in the history of the universe had happened. Christ had defeated death. The door which had always been locked had for the very first time been forced open. This is something quite distinct from mere ghost-survival. I don't mean that they disbelieved in ghost survival. On the contrary, they believed in it so firmly that, on more than one occasion, Christ had had to assure them that He was *not* a ghost. The point is that while believing in survival they yet regarded the Resurrection as something totally different and new. The Resurrection narratives are not a picture of survival after death; they record how a totally new mode of being has arisen in the universe. Something new had appeared in the universe: as new as the first coming of organic life. This Man, after death, does not get divided into "ghost" and "corpse." A new mode of being has arisen. That is the story. What are we going to make of it?

The question is, I suppose, whether any hypothesis covers the facts so well as the Christian hypothesis. That hypothesis is that God has come down into the created universe, down to manhood—and come up again, pulling it up with Him. The alternative hypothesis is not legend, nor exaggeration, nor the apparitions of a ghost. It is either lunacy or lies. Unless one can take the second alternative (and I can't) one turns to the Christian theory.

"What are we to make of Christ?" There is no question of what we can make of Him, it is entirely a question of what He intends to make of us. You must accept or reject the story.

The things He says are very different from what any other teacher has said. Others say, "This is the truth about the universe. This is the way you ought to go," but He says, "*I* am the Truth, and the Way, and the Life." He says, "No man can reach absolute reality, except through Me. Try to retain your own life and you will be inevitably ruined. Give yourself away and you will be saved." He says, "If you are ashamed of Me, if, when you hear this call, you turn the other way, I also will look the other way when I come again as God without disguise. If anything whatever is keeping you from God and from Me, whatever it is, throw it away. If it is your eye, pull it out. If it is your hand, cut it off. If you put yourself first you will be last. Come to Me everyone who is carrying a heavy load, I will set that right. Your sins, all of them, are wiped out. I can do that. I am Rebirth, I am Life. Eat Me, drink Me, I am your Food. And finally, do not be afraid, I have overcome the whole universe." That is the issue.

16.

DANGERS OF
NATIONAL REPENTANCE

THE IDEA OF NATIONAL REPENTANCE SEEMS AT FIRST SIGHT to provide such an edifying contrast to that national self-righteousness of which England is so often accused and with which she entered (or is said to have entered) the last war, that a Christian naturally turns to it with hope. Young Christians especially—last-year undergraduates and first-year curates— are turning to it in large numbers. They are ready to believe that England bears part of the guilt for the present war, and ready to admit their own share in the guilt of England. What that share is, I do not find it easy to determine. Most of these young men were children, and none of them had a vote or the experience which would enable them to use a vote wisely, when England made many of those decisions to which the present disorders could plausibly be traced. Are they, perhaps, repenting what they have in no sense done?

If they are, it might be supposed that their error is very harmless: men fail so often to repent their real sins that the occasional repentance of an imaginary sin might appear almost desirable. But what actually happens (I have watched it happening) to the youthful national penitent is a little more complicated than that. England is not a natural agent, but a civil society. When we speak of England's actions we mean the actions of the British government. The young man who is called upon to repent of England's foreign policy is really being called upon to repent the acts of his neighbor; for a foreign secretary or a cabinet minister is certainly a neighbor. And repentance presupposes condemnation. The first and fatal charm of national repentance is, therefore, the encouragement it gives us to turn from the bitter task of repenting our own sins to the congenial one of bewailing—but, first, of denouncing—the conduct of others. If it were clear to the young that this is what he is doing, no doubt he would remember the law of charity.

Unfortunately the very terms in which national repentance is recommended to him conceal its true nature. By a dangerous figure of speech, he calls the government not "they" but "we." And since, as penitents, we are not encouraged to be charitable to our own sins, nor to give ourselves the benefit of any doubt, a government which is called "we" is *ipso facto* placed beyond the sphere of charity or even of justice. You can say anything you please about it. You can indulge in the popular vice of detraction without restraint, and yet feel all the time that you are practicing contrition. A group of such young penitents will say, "Let us repent our national sins"; what they mean is, "Let us attribute to our neighbor (even our Christian neighbor) in the cabinet, whenever we disagree with him, every abominable motive that Satan can suggest to our fancy."

Such an escape from personal repentance into that tempting region

> Where passions have the privilege to work
> And never hear the sound of their own names,[1]

would be welcome to the moral cowardice of anyone. But it is doubly attractive to the young intellectual. When a man over forty tries to repent the sins of England and to love her enemies, he is attempting something costly; for he was brought up to certain patriotic sentiments which cannot be mortified without a struggle. But an educated man who is now in his twenties usually has no such sentiment to mortify. In art, in literature, in politics, he has been, ever since he can remember, one of an angry and restless minority; he has drunk in almost with his mother's milk a distrust of English statesmen and a contempt for the manners, pleasures, and enthusiasms of his less-educated fellow countrymen. All Christians know that they must forgive their enemies. But "my enemy" primarily means the man whom I am really tempted to hate and traduce. If you listen to young Christian intellectuals talking, you will soon find out who their real enemy is. He seems to have two names— Colonel Blimp and "the businessman." I suspect that the latter usually means the speaker's father, but that is speculation. What is certain is that in asking such people to forgive the Germans and Russians and to open their eyes to the sins of England, you are asking them, not to mortify, but to indulge, their ruling

[1]Wordsworth, *The Prelude*, bk. XI, line 230.

passion. I do not mean that what you are asking them is not right and necessary in itself; we must forgive all our enemies or be damned. But it is emphatically not the exhortation which your audience needs. The communal sins which they should be told to repent are those of their own age and class—its contempt for the uneducated, its readiness to suspect evil, its self-righteous provocations of public obloquy, its breaches of the Fifth Commandment.[2] Of these sins I have heard nothing among them. Till I do, I must think their candor toward the national enemy a rather inexpensive virtue. If a man cannot forgive the Colonel Blimp next door whom he has seen, how shall he forgive the dictators whom he hath not seen?

Is it not, then, the duty of the church to preach national repentance? I think it is. But the office—like many others—can be profitably discharged only by those who discharge it with reluctance. We know that a man may have to "hate" his mother for the Lord's sake.[3] The sight of a Christian rebuking his mother, though tragic, may be edifying; but only if we are quite sure that he has been a good son and that, in his rebuke, spiritual zeal is triumphing, not without agony, over strong natural affection. The moment there is reason to suspect that he *enjoys* rebuking her—that he believes himself to be rising above the natural level while he is still, in reality, groveling below it in the unnatural—the spectacle becomes merely disgusting. The hard sayings of our Lord are wholesome to those only who find them hard. There is a terrible chapter in M. Mauriac's *Vie de Jésus*. When the Lord spoke of brother and child against parent, the other disciples were horrified. Not so Judas. He took to it as a duck takes to water: *"Pourquoi cette stupeur?, se demande Judas. . . . Il aime dans le Christ cette vue simple, ce regard de Dieu sur l'horreur humaine."*[4] For there are two states of mind which face the dominical paradoxes without flinching. God guard us from one of them.

[2]"Honor thy father and thy mother; that thy days may be long in the land which the Lord thy God giveth thee." Exodus xx. 12.

[3]Luke xiv. 26: "If any man come to me, and hate not his father, and mother, and wife, and children, and brethren, and sisters, yea, and his own life also, he cannot be my disciple."

[4]Francois Mauriac, *Vie de Jésus* (Paris, 1936), ch. ix. "'Why this stupefaction?' asked Judas. . . . He loved in Christ his simple view of things, his divine glance at human depravity."

17.

TWO WAYS WITH THE SELF

Sᴇʟꜰ-ʀᴇɴᴜɴᴄɪᴀᴛɪᴏɴ ɪs ᴛʜᴏᴜɢʜᴛ ᴛᴏ ʙᴇ, ᴀɴᴅ ɪɴᴅᴇᴇᴅ ɪs, very near the core of Christian ethics. When Aristotle writes in praise of a certain kind of self-love, we may feel, despite the careful distinctions which he draws between the legitimate and the illegitimate *Philautia*,[1] that here we strike something essentially sub-Christian. It is more difficult, however, to decide what we think of St. François de Sales's chapter, *De la douceur envers nous-mêsmes*,[2] where we are forbidden to indulge resentment even against ourselves and advised to reprove even our own faults *avec des remonstrances douces et tranquilles*,[3] feeling more compassion than passion. In the same spirit, Lady Julian of Norwich would have us "loving and peaceable," not only to our "even-Christians," but to "ourself."[4] Even the New Testament bids me love my neighbor "as myself,"[5] which would be a horrible command if the self were simply to be hated. Yet our Lord also says that a true disciple must "hate his own life."[6]

We must not explain this apparent contradiction by saying that self-love is right up to a certain point and wrong beyond that point. The question is not one of degree. There are two kinds of self-hatred which look rather alike in their earlier stages, but of which one is wrong from the beginning and the other right to the end. When Shelley speaks of self-contempt

---

[1]*Nicomachean Ethics*, bk. ix, ch. 8.

[2]Pt. III, ch. ix. "Of Meekness towards Ourselves" in the *Introduction to the Devout Life* (Lyons, 1609).

[3]"with mild and calm remonstrances."

[4]*The Sixteen Revelations of Divine Love*, ch. xlix.

[5]Matthew xix. 19; xxii. 39; Mark xii. 31, 33; Romans xiii. 9; Galatians v. 14; James ii. 8.

[6]Luke xiv. 26; John xii. 25.

119

as the source of cruelty, or when a later poet says that he has
no stomach for the man "who loathes his neighbor as himself,"
they are referring to a very real and very un-Christian hatred
of the self which may make diabolical a man whom common
selfishness would have have left (at least, for a while) merely
animal. The hard-boiled economist or psychologist of our own
day, recognizing the "ideological taint" or Freudian motive in
his own makeup, does not necessarily learn Christian humility.
He may end in what is called a "low view" of all souls, including
his own, which expresses itself in cynicism or cruelty, or both.
Even Christians, if they accept in certain forms the doctrine of
total depravity, are not always free from the danger. The logical
conclusion of the process is the worship of suffering—for
others as well as for the self—which we see, if I read it aright,
in Mr. David Lindsay's *Voyage to Arcturus*, or that extraordinary vacancy which Shakespeare depicts at the end of *Richard
III*. Richard in his agony tries to turn to self-love. But he has
been "seeing through" all emotions so long that he "sees through"
even this. It becomes a mere tautology: "Richard loves Richard;
that is, I am I."[7]

Now, the self can be regarded in two ways. On the one
hand, it is God's creature, an occasion of love and rejoicing;
now, indeed, hateful in condition, but to be pitied and healed.
On the other hand, it is that one self of all others which is
called *I* and *me*, and which on that ground puts forward an
irrational claim to preference. This claim is to be not only
hated, but simply killed; "never," as George MacDonald says,
"to be allowed a moment's respite from eternal death." The
Christian must wage endless war against the clamor of the *ego*
as *ego:* but he loves and approves selves as such, though not
their sins. The very self-love which he has to reject is to him
a specimen of how he ought to feel to all selves; and he may
hope that when he has truly learned (which will hardly be in
this life) to love his neighbor as himself, he may then be able
to love himself as his neighbor: that is, with charity instead of
partiality. The other kind of self-hatred, on the contrary, hates
selves as such. It begins by accepting the special value of the
particular self called *me;* then, wounded in its pride to find that
such a darling object should be so disappointing, it seeks re-
venge, first upon that self, then on all. Deeply egoistic, but

7 *Richard III*, V, iii, 184.

now with an inverted egoism, it uses the revealing argument, "I don't spare myself"—with the implication "then *a fortiori* I need not spare others"—and becomes like the centurion in Tacitus, *immitior quia toleraverat*.[8]

The wrong asceticism torments the self: the right kind kills the selfness. We must die daily: but it is better to love the self than to love nothing, and to pity the self than to pity no one.

[8]*Annals*, Bk. I, sect. xx, line 14. "More relentless because he had endured (it himself)."

18.

ON THE READING
OF OLD BOOKS[1]

THERE IS A STRANGE IDEA ABROAD THAT IN EVERY SUB-
ject the ancient books should be read only by the professionals,
and that the amateur should content himself with the modern
books. Thus I have found as a tutor in English literature that
if the average student wants to find out something about Platonism, the very last thing he thinks of doing is to take a
translation of Plato off the library shelf and read the *Symposium*.
He would rather read some dreary modern book ten times as
long, all about "isms" and influences and only once in twelve
pages telling him what Plato actually said. The error is rather
an amiable one, for it springs from humility. The student is
half afraid to meet one of the great philosophers face to face.
He feels himself inadequate and thinks he will not understand
him. But if he only knew, the great man, just because of his
greatness, is much more intelligible than his modern commen-
tator. The simplest student will be able to understand, if not
all, yet a very great deal of what Plato said; but hardly anyone
can understand some modern books on Platonism. It has always
therefore been one of my main endeavors as a teacher to per-
suade the young that firsthand knowledge is not only more
worth acquiring then secondhand knowledge, but is usually
much easier and more delightful to acquire.

This mistaken preference for the modern books and this
shyness of the old ones is nowhere more rampant than in theology. Wherever you find a little study circle of Christian laity
you can be almost certain that they are studying not St. Luke
or St. Paul or St. Augustine or Thomas Aquinas or Hooker[2]

---

[1]This paper was orginally written and published as an Introduction to
St. Athanasius's *The Incarnation of the Word of God*, trans. by A. Religious
of C.S.M.V. (London, 1944).

[2]Richard Hooker (c. 1554–1600), an Anglican divine.

or Butler,[3] but M. Berdyaev[4] or M. Maritain[5] or Mr. Niebuhr[6] or Miss Sayers[7] or even myself.

Now this seems to me topsy-turvy. Naturally, since I myself am a writer, I do not wish the ordinary reader to read no modern books. But if he must read only the new or only the old, I would advise him to read the old. And I would give him this advice precisely because he is an amateur and therefore much less protected than the expert against the dangers of an exclusive contemporary diet. A new book is still on its trial and the amateur is not in a position to judge it. It has to be tested against the great body of Christian thought down the ages, and all its hidden implications (often unsuspected by the author himself) have to be brought to light. Often it cannot be fully understood without the knowledge of a good many other modern books. If you join at eleven o'clock a conversation which began at eight you will often not see the real bearing of what is said. Remarks which seem to you very ordinary will produce laughter or irritation and you will not see why—the reason, of course, being that the earlier stages of the conversation have given them a special point. In the same way sentences in a modern book which look quite ordinary may be directed "at" some other book; in this way you may be led to accept what you would have indignantly rejected if you knew its real significance. The only safety is to have a standard of plain, central Christianity ("mere Christianity" as Baxter called it) which puts the controversies of the moment in their proper perspective. Such a standard can be acquired only from the old books. It is a good rule, after reading a new book, never to allow yourself another new one till you have read an old one in between. If that is too much for you, you should at least read one old one to every three new ones.

Every age has its own outlook. It is specially good at seeing certain truths and specially liable to make certain mistakes. We all, therefore, need the books that will correct the characteristic mistakes of our own period. And that means the old books.

[3]Joseph Butler (1692–1752), bishop of Durham.

[4]Nicolas Berdyaev (1874–1948), a Russian philosopher and author.

[5]Jacques Maritain (b. 1820), a French Thomist philosopher.

[6]Reinhold Niebuhr (b. 1892), an American theologian.

[7]Dorothy L. Sayers (1893–1957), author of several religious plays and many popular detective stories.

All contemporary writers share to some extent the contemporary outlook—even those, like myself, who seem most opposed to it. Nothing strikes me more when I read the controversies of past ages than the fact that both sides were usually assuming without question a good deal which we should now absolutely deny. They thought that they were as completely opposed as two sides could be, but in fact they were all the time secretly united—united *with* each other and *against* earlier and later ages—by a great mass of common assumptions. We may be sure that the characteristic blindness of the twentieth century—the blindness about which posterity will ask, "But how *could* they have thought that?"—lies where we have never suspected it, and concerns something about which there is untroubled agreement between Hitler and President Roosevelt[8] or between Mr. H. G. Wells and Karl Barth. None of us can fully escape this blindness, but we shall certainly increase it, and weaken our guard against it, if we read only modern books. Where they are true they will give us truths which we half knew already. Where they are false they will aggravate the error with which we are already dangerously ill. The only palliative is to keep the clean sea breeze of the centuries blowing through our minds, and this can be done only by reading old books. Not, of course, that there is any magic about the past. People were no cleverer then than they are now; they made as many mistakes as we. But not the *same* mistakes. They will not flatter us in the errors we are already committing; and their own errors, being now open and palpable, will not endanger us. Two heads are better than one, not because either is infallible, but because they are unlikely to go wrong in the same direction. To be sure, the books of the future would be just as good a corrective as the books of the past, but unfortunately we cannot get at them.

I myself was first led into reading the Christian classics, almost accidentally, as a result of my English studies. Some, such as Hooker, Herbert,[9] Traherne,[10] Taylor[11] and Bunyan,[12] I read because they are themselves great English writers; others,

---

[8]This was written in 1943.

[9]George Herbert (1593–1633), the English poet.

[10]Thomas Traherne (1637–74), an English writer of religious works.

[11]Jeremy Taylor (1613–67), an English divine, best known for his *Holy Living* and *Holy Dying*.

[12]John Bunyan (1628–88), best known for his *Pilgrim's Progress*.

such as Boethius,[13] St. Augustine, Thomas Aquinas, and Dante, because they were "influences." George MacDonald I had found for myself at the age of sixteen and never wavered in my allegiance, though I tried for a long time to ignore his Christianity. They are, you will note, a mixed bag, representative of many churches, climates and ages. And that brings me to yet another reason for reading them. The divisions of Christendom are undeniable and are by some of these writers most fiercely expressed. But if any man is tempted to think—as one might be tempted who read only contemporaries—that "Christianity" is a word of so many meanings that it means nothing at all, he can learn beyond all doubt, by stepping out of his own century, that this is not so. Measured against the ages "mere Christianity" turns out to be no insipid interdenominational transparency, but something positive, self-consistent, and inexhaustible. I know it, indeed, to my cost. In the days when I still hated Christianity,[14] I learned to recognize, like some all too familiar smell, that almost unvarying *something* which met me, now in Puritan Bunyan, now in Anglican Hooker, now in Thomist Dante. It was there (honeyed and floral) in François de Sales;[15] it was there (grave and homely) in Spenser[16] and Walton;[17] it was there (grim but manful) in Pascal[18] and Johnson;[19] there again, with a mild, frightening, paradisial flavor, in Vaughan[20] and Boehme[21] and Traherne. In the urban sobriety of the eighteenth century one was not safe—Law[22] and Butler were two lions in the path. The supposed "paganism" of the Elizabethans could not keep it out; it lay in wait where a man might have supposed himself safest, in the very center of *The*

---

[13]Boethius was born about 470 A.D. and wrote *The Consolation of Philosophy.*

[14]Those who wish to know more about this period should read Lewis's autobiography, *Surprised by Joy* (London, 1955).

[15]François de Sales (1567–1622) is best known for his *Introduction to the Devout Life* and the *Treatise on the Love of God.*

[16]Edmund Spenser (1522?—99), author of *The Faerie Queene.*

[17]Izaak Walton (1593–1683), best known for his *Compleat Angler.*

[18]Blaise Pascal (1623–62), especially noted for his *Pensées.*

[19]Dr. Samuel Johnson (1709–84).

[20]Henry Vaughan (1622–95), an English poet.

[21]Jakob Boehme (1575–1624), a German Lutheran theosophical author.

[22]William Law (1686–1761), whose *Serious Call to a Devout and Holy Life* much influenced Lewis.

Faerie Queene and the *Arcadia*.[23] It was, of course, varied; and yet—after all—so unmistakably the same; recognizable, not to be evaded, the odor which is death to us until we allow it to become life:

> an air that kills
> From yon far country blows.[24]

We are all rightly distressed, and ashamed also, at the divisions of Christendom. But those who have always lived within the Christian fold may be too easily dispirited by them. They are bad, but such people do not know what it looks like from without. Seen from there, what is left intact, despite all the divisions, still appears (as it truly is) an immensely formidable unity. I know, for I saw it; and well our enemies know it. That unity any of us can find by going out of his own age. It is not enough, but it is more than you had thought till then. Once you are well soaked in it, if you then venture to speak, you will have an amusing experience. You will be thought a Papist when you are actually reproducing Bunyan, a pantheist when you are quoting Aquinas, and so forth. For you have now got on to the great level viaduct which crosses the ages and which looks so high from the valleys, so low from the mountains, so narrow compared with the swamps, and so broad compared with the sheep tracks.

The present book is something of an experiment. The translation is intended for the world at large, not only for theological students. If it succeeds, other translations of other great Christian books will presumably follow. In one sense, of course, it is not the first in the field. Translations of the *Theologia Germanica*,[25] the *Imitation*,[26] the *Scale of Perfection*,[27] and the *Revelations* of Lady Julian of Norwich,[28] are already on the

[23]By Sir Philip Sidney (1554–86).

[24]A. E. Housman, *A Shropshire Lad* (London, 1896), stanza 40.

[25]A late-fourteenth-century anonymous mystical treatise.

[26]*The Imitation of Christ*, a manual of spiritual devotion first put into circulation in 1418. The authorship has traditionally been assigned to Thomas à Kempis (c. 1380–1471).

[27]By Walter Hilton (d. 1396), an English mystic.

[28]*The Sixteen Revelations of Divine Love* by Lady Julian of Norwich (c. 1342 –after 1413).

market, and are very valuable, though some of them are not very scholarly. But it will be noticed that these are all books of devotion rather than of doctrine. Now the layman or amateur needs to be instructed as well as to be exhorted. In this age his need for knowledge is particularly pressing. Nor would I admit any sharp division between the two kinds of book. For my own part, I tend to find the doctrinal books often more helpful in devotion than the devotional books, and I rather suspect that the same experience may await many others. I believe that many who find that "nothing happens" when they sit down, or kneel down, to a book of devotion, would find that the heart sings unbidden while they are working their way through a tough bit of theology with a pipe in their teeth and a pencil in their hand.

This is a good translation of a very great book. St. Athanasius has suffered in popular estimation from a certain sentence in the "Athanasian Creed."[29] I will not labor the point that that work is not exactly a creed and was not by St. Athanasius, for I think it is a very fine piece of writing. The words "Which Faith except every one do keep whole and undefiled, without doubt he shall perish everlastingly" are the offense. They are commonly misunderstood. The operative word is *keep;* not *acquire,* or even *believe,* but *keep.* The author, in fact, is not talking about unbelievers, but about deserters, not about those who have never heard of Christ, nor even those who have misunderstood and refused to accept Him, but of those who having really understood and really believed, then allow themselves, under the sway of sloth or of fashion or any other invited confusion to be drawn away into sub-Christian modes of thought. They are a warning against the curious modern assumption that all changes of belief, however brought about, are necessarily exempt from blame.[30] But this is not my immediate concern. I mention "the Creed (commonly called) of St. Athanasius" only to get out of the reader's way what may have been a bogey and to put the true Athanasius in its place. His epitaph is *Athanasius contra mundum,* "Anthanasius against the world." We are proud that our country has more than once stood against the world. Athanasius did the same. He stood for the Trinitarian doctrine, "whole and undefiled," when it looked as if all the civilized world was slipping back from Christianity into the

[29]A profession of faith found in the English Prayer Book.
[30]See Hebrews vi. 4 *et seq.*

religion of Arius[31]—into one of those "sensible" synthetic religions which are so strongly recommended today and which, then as now, included among their devotees many highly cultivated clergymen. It is his glory that he did not move with the times; it is his reward that he now remains when those times, as all times do, have moved away.

When I first opened his *De Incarnatione* I soon discovered by a very simple test that I was reading a masterpiece. I knew very little Christian Greek except that of the New Testament and I had expected difficulties. To my astonishment I found it almost as easy as Xenophon; and only a mastermind could, in the fourth century, have written so deeply on such a subject with such classical simplicity. Every page I read confirmed this impression. His approach to the miracles is badly needed today, for it is the final answer to those who object to them as "arbitrary and meaningless violations of the Laws of Nature."[32] They are here shown to be rather the retelling in capital letters of the same message which Nature writes in her crabbed cursive hand; the very operations one would expect of Him who was so full of life that when He wished to die He had to "borrow death from others." The whole book, indeed, is a picture of the Tree of Life—a sappy and golden book, full of buoyancy and confidence. We cannot, I admit, appropriate all its confidence today. We cannot point to the high virtue of Christian living and the gay, almost mocking courage of Christian martyrdom, as a proof of our doctrines with quite that assurance which Athanasius takes as a matter of course. But whoever may be to blame for that it is not Athanasius.

The translator knows so much more Christian Greek than I that it would be out of place for me to praise her version. But it seems to me to be in the right tradition of English translation. I do not think the reader will find here any of that sawdusty quality which is so common in modern renderings from the ancient languages. That is as much as the English reader will notice; those who compare the version with the original will be able to estimate how much wit and talent is presupposed in such a choice, for example, as "those wiseacres" on the very first page.

[31]Arius (c. 250–c. 336), a champion of subordinationist teaching about the Person of Christ.

[32]A few years after this was written, Lewis himself wrote an admirable defense of miracles in his *Miracles: A Preliminary Study* (London, 1947).

19.

SCRAPS

1

Yes," MY FRIEND SAID. "I DON'T SEE WHY THERE shouldn't be books in heaven. But you will find that your library in heaven contains only some of the books you had on earth." "Which?" I asked. "The ones you gave away or lent." "I hope the lent ones won't still have all the borrowers' dirty thumb marks," said I. "Oh yes they will," said he. "But just as the wounds of the martyrs will have turned into beauties, so you will find that the thumb marks have turned into beautiful illuminated capitals or exquisite marginal woodcuts."

2

"The angels," he said, "have no senses; their experience is purely intellectual and spiritual. That is why we know something about God which they don't. There are particular aspects of His love and joy which can be communicated to a created being only by sensuous experience. Something of God which the seraphim can never quite understand flows into us from the blue of the sky, the taste of honey, the delicious embrace of water whether cold or hot, and even from sleep itself."

3

"You are always dragging me down," said I to my body. "Dragging *you* down!" replied my body. "Well I like that! Who taught me to like tobacco and alcohol? You, of course, with your idiotic adolescent idea of being "grown up." My palate loathed both at first: but you would have your way. Who put

an end to all those angry and revengeful thoughts last night?
Me, of course, by insisting on going to sleep. Who does his
best to keep you from talking too much and eating too much
by giving you dry throats and headaches and indigestion? Eh?"
"And what about sex?" said I. "Yes, what about it?" retorted
the body. "If you and your wretched imagination would leave
me alone I'd give you no trouble. That's soul all over; you
give me orders and then blame me for carrying them out."

4

"Praying for particular things," said I, "always seems to me
like advising God how to run the world. Wouldn't it be wiser
to assume that He knows best?" "On the same principle," said
he, "I suppose you never ask a man next to you to pass the
salt, because God knows best whether you ought to have salt
or not. And I suppose you never take an umbrella, because
God knows best whether you ought to be wet or dry." "That's
quite different," I protested. "I don't see why," said he. "The
odd thing is that He should let us influence the course of events
at all. But since He lets us do it in one way I don't see why
He shouldn't let us do it in the other."

20.

THE DECLINE OF RELIGION

From what I see of junior Oxford at present it would be quite easy to draw opposite conclusions about the religious predicament of what we call "the rising generation," though in reality the undergraduate body includes men and women almost as much divided from one another in age, outlook, and experience as they are divided from the dons. Plenty of evidence can be produced to show that religion is in its last decline among them, or that a revival of interest in religion is one of their most noticeable characteristics. And in fact something that may be called "a decline" and something that may be called "a revival" are both going on. It will be perhaps more useful to attempt to understand both than to try our luck at "spotting the winner."

The "decline of religion" so often lamented (or welcomed) is held to be shown by empty chapels. Now it is quite true that chapels which were full in 1900 are empty in 1946. But this change was not gradual. It occurred at the precise moment when chapel ceased to be compulsory. It was not in fact a decline; it was a precipice. The sixty men who had come because chapel was a little later than "rollers"[1] (its only alternative) came no more; the five Christians remained. The withdrawal of compulsion did not create a new religious situation, but only revealed the situation which had long existed. And this is typical of the "decline in religion" all over England.

In every class and every part of the country the visible

[1] After there came to be a number of non-Anglican students in the Oxford colleges, those students who did not wish to attend the morning chapel service were required to report to the dean five or ten minutes before the service and have their names put on his roll call. Thus the "rollers," who did not go to chapel, had to be up before those who did go. Neither chapel nor roll call is compulsory now.

131

practice of Christianity has grown very much less in the last fifty years. This is often taken to show that the nation as a whole has passed from a Christian to a secular outlook. But if we judge the nineteenth century from the books it wrote, the outlook of our grandfathers (with a very few exceptions) was quite as secular as our own. The novels of Meredith, Trollope, and Thackeray are not written either by or for men who see this world as the vestibule of eternity, who regard pride as the greatest of the sins, who desire to be poor in spirit, and look for a supernatural salvation. Even more significant is the absence from Dickens' *Christmas Carol* of any interest in the Incarnation. Mary, the Magi, and the Angels are replaced by "spirits" of his own invention, and the animals present are not the ox and ass in the stable but the goose and turkey in the poulterer's shop. Most striking of all is the thirty-third chapter of *The Antiquary*, where Lord Glenallan forgives old Elspeth for her intolerable wrong. Glenallan has been painted by Scott as a lifelong penitent and ascetic, a man whose every thought has been for years fixed on the supernatural. But when he has to forgive, no motive of a Christian kind is brought into play: the battle is won by "the generosity of his nature." It does not occur to Scott that his facts, his solitudes, his beads, and his confessor, however useful as romantic "properties," could be effectively connected with a serious action which concerns the plot of the book.

I am anxious here not to be misunderstood. I do not mean that Scott was not a brave, generous, honorable man and a glorious writer. I mean that in his work, as in that of most of his contemporaries, only secular and natural values are taken seriously. Plato and Virgil are, in that sense, nearer to Christianity than they.

Thus the "decline of religion" becomes a very ambiguous phenomenon. One way of putting the truth would be that the religion which has declined was not Christianity. It was a vague theism with a strong and virile ethical code, which, far from standing over against the "world," was absorbed into the whole fabric of English institutions and sentiment and therefore demanded churchgoing as (at best) a part of loyalty and good manners as (at worst) a proof of respectability. Hence a social pressure, like the withdrawal of the compulsion, did not create a new situation. The new freedom first allowed accurate observations to be made. When no man goes to church except because he seeks Christ the number of actual believers can at last be discovered. It should be added that this new freedom was partly caused by the very conditions which it revealed. If the various anticlerical and antitheistic forces at work in the nineteenth century had had to attack a solid phalanx of radical Christians the story might have been different. But mere "religion"—"morality tinged with emotion," "what a man does with his solitude," "the religion of all good men"—has little power of resistance. It is not good at saying No.

The decline of "religion," thus understood, seems to me in some ways a blessing. At the very worst it makes the issue clear. To the modern undergraduate Christianity is, at least, one of the intellectual options. It is, so to speak, on the agenda: it can be discussed, and a conversion may follow. I can remember times when this was much more difficult. "Religion" (as distinct from Christianity) was too vague to be discussed ("too sacred to be lightly mentioned") and so mixed up with sentiment and good form as to be one of the embarrassing subjects. If it had to be spoken of, it was spoken of in a hushed, medical voice. Something of the shame of the Cross is, and ought to be, irremovable. But the merely social and sentimental embarrassment is gone. The fog of "religion" has lifted; the positions and numbers of both armies can be observed; and real shooting is now possible.

The decline of "religion" is no doubt a bad thing for the "world." By it all the things that made England a fairly happy country are, I suppose, endangered: the comparative purity of her public life, the comparative humanity of her police, and the possibility of some mutal respect and kindness between political opponents. But I am not clear that it makes conversions to Christianity rarer or more difficult: rather the reverse. It makes the choice more unescapable. When the Round Table is broken every man must follow either Galahad or Mordred: middle things are gone.

So much for the decline of religion; now for a Christian revival. Those who claim that there is such a revival would point to the success (I mean success in the sense that it can be tested by sales) of several explicitly and even violently Christian writers, the apparent popularity of lectures on theological subjects, and the brisk atmosphere of not unfriendly discussion on them in which we live. They point, in fact, to what I have heard described as "the highbrow Christian racket." It is difficult to describe the phenomenon in quite neutral terms: but perhaps no one would deny that Christianity is now "on the map" among the younger *intelligentsia* as it was not, say, in 1920. Only freshmen now talk as if the anti-Christian position were self-evident. The days of "simple unfaith" are as dead as those of "simple faith."

At this those who are on the same side as myself are quite properly pleased. We have cause to give thanks: and the comments which I have to add proceed, I hope, not from a natural middle-aged desire to pour cold water into any soup within reach, but only from a desire to forestall, and therefore to disarm, possible disappointments.

In the first place, it must be admitted by anyone who accepts Christianity, that an increased interest in it, or even a growing measure of intellectual assent to it, is a very different thing from the conversion of England or even of a single soul. Conversion requires an alteration of the will, and an alteration which, in the last resort, does not occur without the intervention of the supernatural. I do not in the least agree with those who therefore conclude that the spread of an intellectual (and imaginative) climate favorable to Christianity is useless. You do not prove munition workers useless by showing that they cannot themselves win battles, however proper this reminder would be if they attempted to claim the honor due to fighting men. If the intellectual climate is such that, when a man comes to the crisis at which he must either accept or reject Christ, his reason and imagination are not on the wrong side, then his conflict will be fought out under favorable conditions. Those who help to produce and spread such a climate are therefore doing useful work: and yet no such great matter after all. Their share is a modest one; and it is always possible that nothing—nothing whatever—may come of it. Far higher than they stands that character whom, to the best of my knowledge, the present Christian movement has not yet produced—the *preacher* in the full sense, the evangelist, the man on fire, the man who infects. The propagandist, the apologist, only represents John Baptist: the preacher represents the Lord Himself. He will be sent—or else he will not. But unless he comes we mere Christian intellectuals will not effect very much. That does not mean we should down tools.

In the second place we must remember that a widespread and lively interest in a subject is precisely what we call a fashion. And it is the nature of fashions not to last. The present Christian movement may, or may not, have a long run ahead of it. But sooner or later it must lose the public ear; in a place like Oxford such changes are extraordinarily rapid. Bradley and the other idealists fell in a few terms, the Douglas scheme even more suddenly, the Vorticists overnight.[2] (Who now remembers pogo? Who now reads *Childermass*?[3]) Whatever in our present success mere fashion has given us, mere fashion will presently withdraw. The real conversions will remain: but nothing else will. In that sense we may be on the brink of a real and permanent Christian revival: but it will work slowly and obscurely and in small groups. The present sunshine (if I may so call it) is certainly temporary. The grain must be got into the barns before the wet weather comes.

This mutability is the fate of all movements, fashions, intellectual climates, and the like. But a Christian movement is also up against something sterner than the mere fickleness of taste. We have not yet had (at least in junior Oxford) any really bitter opposition. But if we have many more successes, this will certainly appear. The enemy has not yet thought it worth while to fling his whole weight against us. But he soon will. This happens in the history of every Christian movement, beginning with the ministry of Christ Himself. At first it is welcome to all who have no special reason for opposing it: at this stage he who is not against it is for it. What men notice is its difference from those aspects of the world which they already dislike. But later on, as the real meaning of the Christian claim becomes apparent, its demand for total surrender, the sheer chasm between Nature and Supernature, men are increasingly "offended." Dislike, terror, and finally hatred succeed: none who will not give it what it asks (and it asks all) can endure it: all who are not with it are against it. That is why we must cherish no picture of the present intellectual movement simply growing and spreading and finally reclaiming millions by sweet resonableness. Long before it became as important as that the real opposition would have begun, and to be on the Christian side would be costing a man (at the least) his career. But remember, in England the opposition will quite likely be *called*

[2]F. H. Bradley (1846–1924) was a Fellow of Merton College, Oxford, and the author of *Appearance and Reality* (London, 1893). Major C. H. Douglas, a socioeconomist, wrote, among other works, *Social Credit* (London, 1933). The Vorticists were a school of artists of the 1920s.

[3]No one, practically. As far as I can discover, pogo, or the pogo stick, which was invented in 1922, is a stilt with a spring on which the player jumps about. *Childermass* is by P. Wyndham Lewis (London, 1928).

Christianity (or Christo-democracy, or British Christianity, or something of that kind).

I think—but how should I know?—that all is going reasonably well. But it is early days. Neither our armor nor our enemies' is yet engaged. Combatants always tend to imagine that the war is further on than it really is.

21.

VIVISECTION

It is the rarest thing in the world to hear a rational discussion of vivisection. Those who disapprove of it are commonly accused of "sentimentality," and very often their arguments justify the accusation. They paint pictures of pretty little dogs on dissecting tables. But the other side lie open to exactly the same charge. They also often defend the practice by drawing pictures of suffering women and children whose pain can be relieved (we are assured) only by the fruits of vivisection. The one appeal, quite as clearly as the other, is addressed to emotion, to the particular emotion we call pity. And neither appeal proves anything. If the thing is right—and if right at all, it is a duty—then pity for the animal is one of the temptations we must resist in order to perform that duty. If the thing is wrong, then pity for human suffering is precisely the temptation which will most probably lure us into doing that wrong thing. But the real question—whether it is right or wrong—remains meanwhile just where it was.

A rational discussion of this subject begins by inquiring whether pain is, or is not, an evil. If it is not, then the case against vivisection falls. But then so does the case for vivisection. If it is not defended on the ground that it reduces human suffering, on what ground can it be defended? And if pain is not an evil, why should human suffering be reduced? We must therefore assume as a basis for the whole discussion that pain is an evil, otherwise there is nothing to be discussed.

Now if pain is an evil then the infliction of pain, considered in itself, must clearly be an evil act. But there are such things as necessary evils. Some acts which would be bad, simply in themselves, may be excusable and even laudable when they are necessary means to a greater good. In saying that the infliction of pain, simply in itself, is bad, we are not saying that pain ought never to be inflicted. Most of us think that it can

137

rightly be inflicted for a good purpose—as in dentistry or just and reformatory punishment. The point is that it always requires justification. On the man whom we find inflicting pain rests the burden of showing why an act which in itself would be simply bad is, in those particular circumstances, good. If we find a man giving pleasure it is for us to prove (if we criticize him) that his action is wrong. But if we find a man inflicting pain it is for him to prove that his action is right. If he cannot, he is a wicked man.

Now vivisection can only be defended by showing it to be right that one species should suffer in order that another species should be happier. And here we come to the parting of the ways. The Christian defender and the ordinary "scientific" (i.e. naturalistic) defender of vivisection, have to take quite different lines.

The Christian defender, especially in the Latin countries, is very apt to say that we are entitled to do anything we please to animals because they "have no souls." But what does this mean? If it means that animals have no consciousness, then how is this known? They certainly behave as if they had, or at least the higher animals do. I myself am inclined to think that far fewer animals than is supposed have what we should recognize as consciousness. But that is only an opinion. Unless we know on other grounds that vivisection is right we must not take the moral risk of tormenting them on a mere opinion. On the other hand, the statement that they "have no souls" may mean that they have no moral responsibilities and are not immortal. But the absence of "soul" in that sense makes the infliction of pain upon them not easier but harder to justify. For it means that animals cannot deserve pain, nor profit morally by the discipline of pain, nor be recompensed by happiness in another life for suffering in this. Thus all the factors which render pain more tolerable or make it less totally evil in the case of human beings will be lacking in the beasts. "Soullessness," insofar as it is relevant to the question at all, is an argument against vivisection.

The only rational line for the Christian vivisectionist to take is to say that the superiority of man over beast is a real objective fact, guaranteed by revelation, and that the propriety of sacrificing beast to man is a logical consequence. We are "worth more than many sparrows,"[1] and in saying this we are not

[1] Matthew x. 31.

merely expressing a natural preference for our own species simply because it is our own but conforming to a hierarchical order created by God and really present in the universe whether any one acknowledges it or not. The position may not be satisfactory. We may fail to see how a benevolent Deity could wish us to draw such conclusions from the hierarchical order He has created. We may find it difficult to formulate a human right of tormenting beasts in terms which would not equally imply an angelic right of tormenting men. And we may feel that though objective superiority is rightly claimed for man, yet that very superiority ought partly to *consist in* not behaving like a vivisector: that we ought to prove ourselves better than the beasts precisely by the fact of acknowledging duties to them which they do not acknowledge to us. But on all these questions different opinions can be honestly held. If on grounds of our real, divinely ordained, superiority a Christian pathologist thinks it right to vivisect, and does so with scrupulous care to avoid the least dram or scruple of unnecessary pain, in a trembling awe at the responsibility which he assumes, and with a vivid sense of the high mode in which human life must be lived if it is to justify the sacrifices made for it, then (whether we agree with him or not) we can respect his point of view.

But of course the vast majority of vivisectors have no such theological background. They are most of them naturalistic and Darwinian. Now here, surely, we come up against a very alarming fact. The very same people who will most contemptuously brush aside any consideration of animal suffering if it stands in the way of "research" will also, on another context, most vehemently deny that there is any radical difference between man and the other animals. On the naturalistic view the beasts are at bottom just the same *sort* of thing as ourselves. Man is simply the cleverest of the anthropoids. All the grounds on which a Christian might defend vivisection are thus cut from under our feet. We sacrifice other species to our own not because our own has any objective metaphysical privilege over others, but simply because it is ours. It may be very natural to have this loyalty to our own species, but let us hear no more from the naturalists about the "sentimentality" of antivivisectionists. If loyalty to our own species, preference for man simply because we are men, is not a sentiment, then what is? It may be a good sentiment or a bad one. But a sentiment it certainly is. Try to base it on logic and see what happens!

But the most sinister thing about modern vivisection is this. If a mere sentiment justifies cruelty, why stop at a sentiment for the whole human race? There is also a sentiment for the white man against the black, for a *Herrenvolk* against the non-Aryans, for "civilized" or "progressive" peoples against "savage" or "backward" peoples. Finally, for our own country, party, or class against others. Once the old Christian idea of a total difference in kind between man beast has been abandoned, then no argument for experiments on animals can be found which is not also an argument for experiments on inferior men. If we cut up beasts simply because they cannot prevent us and because we are backing our own side in the struggle for existence, it is only logical to cut up imbeciles, criminals, enemies, or capitalists for the same reasons. Indeed, experiments on men have already begun. We all hear that Nazi scientists have done them. We all suspect that our own scientists may begin to do so, in secret, at any moment.

The alarming thing is that the vivisectors have won the first round. In the nineteenth and eighteenth century a man was not stamped as a "crank" for protesting against vivisection. Lewis Carroll protested, if I remember his famous letter correctly, on the very same ground which I have just used.[2] Dr. Johnson— a man whose mind had as much *iron* in it as any man's— protested in a note on *Cymbeline* which is worth quoting in full. In Act I, scene v, the Queen explains to the Doctor that she wants poisons to experiment on "such creatures as We count not worth the hanging,—but none human."[3] The Doctor replies:

> Your Highness
> Shall from this practice but make hard your heart.[4]

Johnson comments: "The thought would probably have been more amplified, had our author lived to be shocked with such experiments as have been published in later times, by a race of men that have practiced tortures without pity, and related them without shame, and are yet suffered to erect their heads among human beings."[5]

[2]"Vivisection as a Sign of the Times," *The Works of Lewis Carroll*, ed. Roger Lancelyn Green (London, 1965), pp. 1089–92. See also "Some Popular Fallacies about Vivisection," *ib.*, pp. 1092–1100.

[3]Shakespeare, *Cymbeline*, I, v, 19–20.

[4]*Ibid.*, 23.

[5]*Johnson on Shakespeare: Essays and Notes Selected and Set Forth with an Introduction* by Sir Walter Raleigh (London, 1908), p. 181.

The words are his, not mine, and in truth we hardly dare in these days to use such calmly stern language. The reason why we do not dare is that the other side has in fact won. And though cruelty even to beasts is an important matter, their victory is symptomatic of matters more important still. The victory of vivisection marks a great advance in the triumph of ruthless, nonmoral utilitarianism over the old world of ethical law; a triumph in which we, as well as animals, are already the victims, and of which Dachau and Hiroshima mark the more recent achievements. In justifying cruelty to animals we put ourselves also on the animal level. We choose the jungle and must abide by our choice.

You will notice I have spent no time in discussing what actually goes on in the laboratories. We shall be told, of course, that there is surprisingly little cruelty. That is a question with which, at present, I have nothing to do. We must first decide what should be allowed: after that it is for the police to discover what is already being done.

22.

MODERN TRANSLATIONS OF THE BIBLE

IT IS POSSIBLE THAT THE READER WHO OPENS THIS VOLUME[1] on the counter of a book shop may ask himself why we need a new translation of any part of the Bible, and, if of any, why of the Epistles. "Do we not already possess," it may be said, "in the Authorized Version the most beautiful rendering which any language can boast?" Some people whom I have met go even further and feel that a modern translation is not only unnecessary but even offensive. They cannot bear to see the time-honored words altered; it seems to them irreverent.

There are several answers to such people. In the first place the kind of objection which they feel to a new translation is very like the objection which was once felt to any English translation at all. Dozens of sincerely pious people in the sixteenth century shuddered at the idea of turning the time-honored Latin of the Vulgate into our common and (as they thought) "barbarous" English. A sacred truth seemed to them to have lost its sanctity when it was stripped of the polysyllabic Latin, long heard at Mass and at Hours, and put into "language such as men do use"—language steeped in all the commonplace associations of the nursery, the inn, the stable, and the street. The answer then was the same as the answer now. The only kind of sanctity which Scripture can lose (or, at least, New Testament scripture) by being modernized is an accidental kind which it never had for its writers or its earliest readers. The New Testament in the original Greek is not a work of literary art: it is not written in a solemn, ecclesiastical language, it is written in the sort of Greek which was spoken over the Eastern Mediterranean after Greek had become an international lan-

[1]This essay was originally published as an Introduction to J. B. Philips's *Letters to Young Churches: A Translation of the New Testament Epistles (London, 1947).*

guage and therefore lost its real beauty and subtlety. In it we see Greek used by people who have no real feeling for Greek words because Greek words are not the words they spoke when they were children. It is a sort of "basic" Greek; a language without roots in the soil, a utilitarian, commercial, and administrative language. Does this shock us? It ought not to, except as the Incarnation itself ought to shock us. The same divine humility which decreed that God should become a baby at a peasant-woman's breast, and later an arrested field preacher in the hands of the Roman police, decreed also that He should be preached in a vulgar, prosaic, and unliterary language. If you can stomach the one, you can stomach the other. The Incarnation is in that sense an irreverent doctrine: Christianity, in that sense, an incurably irreverent religion. When we expect that it should have come before the world in all the beauty that we now feel in the Authorized Version we are as wide of the mark as the Jews were in expecting that the Messiah would come as a great earthly king. The real sancitity, the real beauty and sublimity of the New Testament (as of Christ's life) are of a different sort: miles deeper or *further in*.

In the second place, the Authorized Version has ceased to be a good (that is, a clear) translation. It is no longer modern English: the meanings of words have changed. The same antique glamour which has made it (in the superficial sense) so "beautiful," so "sacred," so "comforting," and so "inspiring," has also made it in many places unintelligible. Thus where St. Paul says "I know nothing against myself," it translates "I know nothing by myself."[2] That was a good translation (though even then rather old-fashioned) in the sixteenth century: to the modern reader it means either nothing, or something quite different from what St. Paul said. The truth is that if we are to have translation at all we must have periodical retranslation. There is no such thing as translating a book into another language once and for all, for a language is a changing thing. If your son is to have clothes it is no good buying him a suit once and for all: he will grow out of it and have to be reclothed.

And finally, though it may seem a sour paradox—we must sometimes get away from the Authorized Version, if for no other reason, simply *because* it is so beautiful and so solemn. Beauty exalts, but beauty also lulls. Early associations endear

[2] I Corinthians iv. 4.

but they also confuse. Through that beautiful solemnity the transporting or horrifying realities of which the book tells may come to us blunted and disarmed and we may only sigh with tranquil veneration when we ought to be burning with shame or struck dumb with terror or carried out of ourselves by ravishing hopes and adorations. Does the word "scourged"[3] really come home to us like "flogged"? Does "mocked him"[4] sting like "jeered at him"?

We ought therefore to welcome all new translations (when they are made by sound scholars) and most certainly those who are approaching the Bible for the first time will be wise not to begin with the Authorized Version—except perhaps for the historical books of the Old Testament where its archaisms suit the sagalike material well enough. Among modern translations those of Dr. Moffatt[5] and Monsignor Knox[6] seem to me particularly good. The present volume concentrates on the epistles and furnishes more help to the beginner: its scope is different. The preliminary abstracts to each letter will be found especially useful, and the reader who has not read the letters before might do well to begin by reading and reflecting on these abstracts at some length before he attempts to tackle the text. It would have saved me a great deal of labor if this book had come into my hands when I first seriously began to try to discover what Christianity was.

For a man who wants to make that discovery must face the Epistles. And whether we like it or not, most of them are by St. Paul. He is the Christian author whom no one can bypass.

A most astonishing misconception has long dominated the modern mind on the subject of St. Paul. It is to this effect: that Jesus preached a kindly and simple religion (found in the Gospels) and that St. Paul afterwards corrupted it into a cruel and complicated religion (found in the Epistles). This is really quite untenable. All the most terrifying texts come from the mouth of our Lord: all the texts on which we can base such warrant as we have for hoping that all men will be saved come from

[3]John xix. 1.

[4]Matthew xxvii. 29; Mark xv. 20; Luke xxii. 63; xxiii. 11, 36.

[5]James Moffatt (1870–1944), whose translation of the New Testament appeared in 1913, his translation of the Old Testament in 1924, and the whole being revised in 1935.

[6]Ronald A. Knox (1888–1957) published a translation of the New Testament in 1945, and a translation of the Old Testament in 1949.

St. Paul. If it could be proved that St. Paul altered the teaching of his Master in any way, he altered it in exactly the opposite way to that which is popularly supposed. But there is no real evidence for a pre-Pauline doctrine different from St. Paul's. The Epistles are, for the most part, the earliest Christian documents we possess. The Gospels come later. They are not "the gospel," the statement of the Christian belief. They were written for those who had already been converted, who had already accepted "the gospel." They leave out many of the "complications" (that is, the theology) because they are intended for readers who have already been instructed in it. In that sense the Epistles are more primitive and more central than the Gospels—though not, of course, than the great events which the Gospels recount. God's act (the Incarnation, the Crucifixion, and the Resurrection) comes first: the earliest theological analysis of it comes in the Epistles: then, when the generation who had known the Lord was dying out, the Gospels were composed to provide for believers a record of the great act and of some of the Lord's sayings. The ordinary popular conception has put everything upside down. Nor is the cause far to seek. In the earlier history of every rebellion there is a stage at which you do not yet attack the king in person. You say, "The king is all right. It is his ministers who are wrong. They misrepresent him and corrupt all his plans—which, I'm sure, are good plans if only the ministers would let them take effect." And the first victory consists in beheading a few ministers: only at a later stage do you go on and behead the king himself. In the same way, the nineteenth-century attack on St. Paul was really only a stage in the revolt against Christ. Men were not ready in large numbers to attack Christ Himself. They made the normal first move—that of attacking one of His principal ministers. Everything they disliked in Christianity was therefore attributed to St. Paul. It was unfortunate that their case could not impress anyone who had really read the Gospels and the Epistles with attention: but apparently few people had, and so the first victory was won. St. Paul was impeached and banished and the world went on to the next step—the attack on the King Himself. But to those who wish to know what St. Paul and his fellow teachers really said the present volume will give very great help.

23.

GOD IN THE DOCK

I HAVE BEEN ASKED TO WRITE ABOUT THE DIFFICULTIES WHICH a man must face in trying to present the Christian faith to modern unbelievers. That is too wide a subject for my capacity or even for the scope of an article. The difficulties vary as the audience varies. The audience may be of this or that nation, may be children or adults, learned or ignorant. My own experience is of English audiences only, and almost exclusively of adults. It has, in fact, been mostly of men (and women) serving in the R.A.F.[1] This has meant that while very few of them have been learned in the academic sense of that word, a large number of them have had a smattering of elementary practical science, have been mechanics, electricians, or wireless operators; for the rank and file of the R.A.F. belong to what may almost be called "the intelligentsia of the proletariat." I have also talked to students at the universities. These strict limitations in my experience must be kept in mind by the readers. How rash it would be to generalize from such an experience I myself discovered on the single occasion when I spoke to soldiers. It became at once clear to me that the level of intelligence in our army is very much lower than in the R.A.F. and that quite a different approach was required.

The first thing I learned from addressing the R.A.F. was that I had been mistaken in thinking materialism to be our only considerable adversary. Among the English "intelligentsia of the proletariat," materialism is only among many non-Christian creeds—theosophy, spiritualism, British Israelitism, etc. England has, of course, always been the home of "cranks"; I see no sign that they are diminishing. Consistent Marxism I very seldom met. Whether this is because it is very rare, or because men speaking in the presence of their officers concealed it, or

[1]Royal Air Force.

because Marxists did not attend the meetings at which I spoke, I have no means of knowing. Even where Christianity was professed, it was often much tainted with pantheistic elements. Strict and well-informed Christian statements, when they occurred at all, usually came from Roman Catholics or from members of extreme Protestant sects (e.g. Baptists). My student audiences shared, in a less degree, the theological vagueness I found in the R.A.F., but among them strict and well-informed statements came from Anglo-Catholics and Roman Catholics; seldom, if ever, from Dissenters. The various non-Christian religions mentioned above hardly appeared.

The next thing I learned from the R.A.F. was that the English proletariat is sceptical about history to a degree which academically educated persons can hardly imagine. This, indeed, seems to me to be far the widest cleavage between the learned and unlearned. The educated man habitually, almost without noticing it, sees the present as something that grows out of a long perspective of centuries. In the minds of my R.A.F. hearers this perspective simply did not exist. It seemed to me that they did not really believe that we have any reliable knowledge of historic man. But this was often curiously combined with a conviction that we knew a great deal about prehistoric man: doubtless because prehistoric man is labeled "science" (which is reliable) whereas Napoleon or Julius Caesar is labeled as "history" (which is not). Thus a pseudoscientific picture of the "caveman" and a picture of "the present" filled almost the whole of their imaginations; between these, there lay only a shadowy and unimportant region in which the phantasmal shapes of Roman soldiers, stagecoaches, pirates, knights-in-armor, highwaymen, etc., moved in a mist. I had supposed that if my hearers disbelieved the Gospels, they would do so because the Gospels recorded miracles. But my impression is that they disbelieved them simply because they dealt with events that happened a long time ago: that they would be almost as incredulous of the battle of Actium as of the Resurrection—and for the same reason. Sometimes this scepticism was defended by the argument that all books before the invention of printing must have been copied and recopied till the text was changed beyond recognition. And here came another surprise. When their historical scepticism took that rational form, it was sometimes easily allayed by the mere statement that there existed a "science called textual criticism" which gave us a reasonable assurance that some ancient texts were accurate. This ready acceptance of the authority of specialists is significant, not only for its ingenuousness but also because it underlines a fact of which my experiences have on the whole convinced me; i.e. that very little of the opposition we meet is inspired by malice or suspicion. It is based on genuine doubt, and often on doubt that is reasonable in the state of the doubter's knowledge.

My third discovery is of a difficulty which I suspect to be more acute in England than elsewhere. I mean the difficulty occasioned by language. In all societies, no doubt, the speech of the vulgar differs from that of the learned. The English language with its double vocabulary (Latin and native), English manners (with their boundless indulgence to slang, even in polite circles) and English culture which allows nothing like the French Academy, make the gap unusually wide. There are almost two languages in the country. The man who wishes to speak to the uneducated in English must learn their language. It is not enough that he should abstain from using what he regards as "hard words." He must discover empirically what words exist in the language of his audience and what they mean in that language: e.g. that *potential* means not "possible" but " power," that *creature* means not creature but "animal," that *primitive* means "rude" or "clumsy," that *rude* means (often) "scabrous," "obscene," that the *Immaculate Conception* (except in the mouths of Roman Catholics) means "the Virgin Birth." A *Being* means "a personal being": a man who said to me "I believe in the Holy Ghost, but I don't think it is a being," meant: "I believe there is such a being, but that it is not personal." On the other hand, *personal* sometimes means "corporeal." When an uneducated Englishman says that he believes "in God, but not in a personal God," he may mean simply and solely that he is not an anthropomorphist in the strict and original sense of that word. *Abstract* seems to have two meanings: (a) "immaterial," (b) "vague," obscure, and unpractical. Thus arithmetic is not, in their language, an "abstract" science. *Practical* means often "economic" or "utilitarian." *Morality* nearly always means "chastity": thus in their language the sentence "I do not say that this woman is immoral but I do say that she is a thief," would not be nonsense, but would mean: "She is chaste but dishonest." *Christian* has an eulogistic rather than a descriptive sense: e.g. "Christian standards" means simply "high moral standards." The proposition "So and so is not a

Christian" would only be taken to be a criticism of his behavior, never to be merely a statement of his beliefs. It is also important to notice that what would seem to the learned to be the harder of two words may in fact, to the uneducated, be the easier. Thus it was recently proposed to emend a prayer used in the Church of England that magistrates "may truly and indifferently administer justice" to "may truly and impartially administer justice." A country priest told me that his sexton understood and could accurately explain the meaning of "indifferently" but had no idea of what "impartially" meant.

The popular English language, then, simply has to be learned by him who would preach to the English: just as a missionary learns Bantu before preaching to the Bantus. This is the more necessary because once the lecture or discussion has begun, digressions on the meaning of words tend to bore uneducated audiences and even to awaken distrust. There is no subject in which they are less interested than philology. Our problem is often simply one of translation. Every examination for ordinands ought to include a passage from some standard theological work for translation into the vernacular. The work is laborious but it is immediately rewarded. By trying to translate our doctrines into vulgar speech we discover how much we understand them ourselves. Our failure to translate may sometimes be due to our ignorance of the vernacular; much more often it exposes the fact that we do not exactly know what we mean.

Apart from this linguistic difficulty, the greatest barrier I have met is the almost total absence from the minds of my audience of any sense of sin. This has struck me more forcibly when I spoke to the R.A.F. than when I spoke to students: whether (as I believe) the proletariat is more self-righteous than other classes, or whether educated people are cleverer at concealing their pride, this creates for us a new situation. The early Christian preachers could assume in their hearers, whether Jews, *Metuentes,* or Pagans, a sense of guilt. (That this was common among Pagans is shown by the fact that both Epicureanism and the mystery religions both claimed, though in different ways, to assuage it.) Thus the Christian message was in those days unmistakably the *Evangelium,* the Good News. It promised healing to those who knew they were sick. We have to convince our hearers of the unwelcome diagnosis before we can expect them to welcome the news of the remedy.

The ancient man approached God (or even the gods) as the

accused person approaches his judge. For the modern man the roles are reversed. He is the judge: God is in the dock. He is quite a kindly judge: if God should have a reasonable defense for being the god who permits war, poverty, and disease, he is ready to listen to it. The trial may even end in God's acquittal. But the important thing is that man is on the bench and God in the dock.

It is generally useless to try to combat this attitude, as older preachers did, by dwelling on sins like drunkenness and unchastity. The modern proletariat is not drunken. As for fornication, contraceptives have made a profound difference. As long as this sin might socially ruin a girl by making her the mother of a bastard, most men recognized the sin against charity which it involved, and their consciences were often troubled by it. Now that it need have no such consequences, it is not, I think, generally felt to be a sin at all. My own experience suggests that if we can awake the conscience of our hearers at all, we must do so in quite different directions. We must talk of conceit, spite, jealousy, cowardice, meanness, etc. But I am very far from believing that I have found the solution of this problem.

Finally, I must add that my own work has suffered very much from the incurable intellectualism of my approach. The simple, emotional appeal ("Come to Jesus") is still often successful. But those who, like myself, lack the gift for making it, had better not attempt it.

24.

CROSS-EXAMINATION

[The following is an interview with C. S. Lewis, held on May 7, 1963, in Lewis's rooms in Magdalene College, Cambridge. The interviewer is Mr. Sherwood E. Wirt of the Billy Graham Evangelistic Association Ltd.]

Mr Wirt:

Professor Lewis, if you had a young friend with some interest in writing on Christian subjects, how would you advise him to prepare himself?

Lewis:

I would say if a man is going to write on chemistry, he learns chemistry. The same is true of Christianity. But to speak of the craft itself, I would not know how to advise a man how to write. It is a matter of talent and interest. I believe he must be strongly moved if he is to become a writer. Writing is like a "lust," or like "scratching when you itch." Writing comes as a result of a very strong impulse, and when it does come, I for one must get it out.

Mr Wirt:

Can you suggest an approach that would spark the creation of a body of Christian literature strong enough to influence our generation?

Lewis:

There is no formula in these matters. I have no recipe, no tablets. Writers are trained in so many individual ways that it is not for us to prescribe. Scripture itself is not systematic; the New Testament shows the greatest variety. God has shown us that he can use any instrument. Balaam's ass, you remember,

151

preached a very effective sermon in the midst of his "hee-haws."[1]

Mr Wirt:

A light touch has been characteristic of your writings, even when you are dealing with heavy theological themes. Would you say there is a key to the cultivation of such an attitude?

Lewis:

I believe this is a matter of temperament. However, I was helped in achieving this attitude by my studies of the literary men of the Middle Ages, and by the writings of G. K. Chesterton. Chesterton, for example, was not afraid to combine serious Christian themes with buffoonery. In the same way, the miracle plays of the Middle Ages would deal with a sacred subject such as the nativity of Christ, yet would combine it with a farce.

Mr Wirt:

Should Christian writers, then, in your opinion, attempt to be funny?

Lewis:

No. I think that forced jocularities on spiritual subjects are an abomination, and the attempts of some religious writers to be humorous are simply appalling. Some people write heavily, some write lightly. I prefer the light approach because I believe there is a great deal of false reverence about. There is too much solemnity and intensity in dealing with sacred matters; too much speaking in holy tones.

Mr Wirt:

But is not solemnity proper and conductive to a sacred atmosphere?

Lewis:

Yes and no. There is a difference between a private devotional life and a corporate one. Solemnity is proper in church, but things that are proper in church are not necessarily proper outside, and vice versa. For example, I can say a prayer while

[1] Numbers xxii. 1–35.

washing my teeth, but that does not mean I should wash my teeth in church.

Mr Wirt:

What is your opinion of the kind of writing being done within the Christian Church today?

Lewis:

A great deal of what is being published by writers in the religious tradition is a scandal and is actually turning people away from the church. The liberal writers who are continually accommodating and whittling down the truth of the Gospel are responsible. I cannot understand how a man can appear in print claiming to disbelieve everything that he presupposes when he puts on the surplice. I feel it is a form of prostitution.

Mr Wirt:

What do you think of the controversial new book, *Honest to God*, by John Robinson, the bishop of Woolwich?

Lewis:

I prefer being honest to being "honest to God."

Mr Wirt:

What Christian writers have helped you?

Lewis:

The contemporary book that has helped me the most is Chesterton's *The Everlasting Man*. Others are Edwyn Bevan's book, *Symbolism and Belief*, and Rudolf Otto's *The Idea of the Holy*, and the plays of Dorothy Sayers.[2]

Mr Wirt:

I believe it was Chesterton who was asked why he became a member of the church, and he replied, "To get rid of my sins."

Lewis:

It is not enough to want to get rid of one's sins. We also need to believe in the one who saves us from our sins. Not

---

[2]Such as *The Man Born to be King* (London, 1943; reprinted Grand Rapids, 1970).

only do we need to recognize that we are sinners; we need to believe in a savior who takes away sin. Matthew Arnold once wrote, "Nor does the being hungry prove that we have bread." Because we are sinners, it does not follow that we are saved.

Mr Wirt:

In your book *Surprised by Joy* you remark that you were brought into the faith kicking and struggling and resentful, with eyes darting in every direction looking for an escape.[3] You suggest that you were compelled, as it were, to become a Christian. Do you feel that you made a decision at the time of your conversion?

Lewis:

I would not put it that way. What I wrote in *Surprised by Joy* was that "before God closed in on me, I was in fact offered what now appears a moment of wholly free choice."[4] But I feel my decision was not so important. I was the object rather than the subject in this affair. I was decided upon. I was glad afterwards at the way it came out, but at the moment what I heard was God saying, "Put down your gun and we'll talk."

Mr Wirt:

That sounds to me as if you came to a very definite point of decision.

Lewis:

Well, I would say that the most deeply compelled action is also the freest action. By that I mean, no part of you is outside the action. It is a paradox. I expressed it in *Surprised by Joy* by saying that I chose, yet it really did not seem possible to do the opposite.[5]

Mr Wirt:

You wrote twenty years ago that "A man who was merely a man and said the sort of things Jesus said would not be a great moral teacher. He would either be a lunatic—on a level with the man who says he is a poached egg—or else he would be the Devil of hell. You must make your choice. Either this

[3](London, 1955), ch. xiv, p. 215.

[4]*Ibid.*, p. 211.

[5]*Ibid.*

man was, and is, the Son of God: or else a madman or something worse. You can shut Him up for a fool, you can spit at Him and kill Him as a demon; or you can fall at His feet and call Him Lord and God. But let us not come with any patronizing nonsense about His being a great human teacher. He has not left that open to us. He did not intend to."[6] Would you say your view of this matter has changed since then?

Lewis:

I would say there is no substantial change.

Mr Wirt:

Would you say that the aim of Christian writing, including your own writing, is to bring about an encounter of the reader with Jesus Christ?

Lewis:

That is not my language, yet it is the purpose I have in view. For example, I have just finished a book on prayer, an imaginary correspondence with someone who raises questions about difficulties in prayer.[7]

Mr Wirt:

How can we foster the encounter of people with Jesus Christ?

Lewis:

You can't lay down any pattern for God. There are many different ways of bringing people into His Kingdom, even some ways that I specially dislike! I have therefore learned to be cautious in my judgment.

But we can block it in many ways. As Christians we are tempted to make unnecessary concessions to those outside the faith. We give in too much. Now, I don't mean that we should run the risk of making a nuisance of ourselves by witnessing at improper times, but there comes a time when we must show that we disagree. We must show our Christian colors, if we are to be true to Jesus Christ. We cannot remain silent or concede everything away.

There is a character in one of my children's stories named

[6] *Mere Christianity* (London, 1952), ch. iii, p. 42.

[7] He is speaking of his *Letters to Malcolm: Chiefly on Prayer* (London, 1964).

Aslan, who says, "I never tell anyone any story except his own."[8] I cannot speak for the way God deals with others; I only know how He deals with me personally. Of course, we are to pray for spiritual awakening, and in various ways we can do something toward it. But we must remember that neither Paul nor Apollos gives the increase.[9] As Charles Williams once said, "The altar must often be built in one place so that the fire may come down in another place."[10]

Mr Wirt:

Professor Lewis, your writings have an unusual quality not often found in discussions of Christian themes. You write as though you enjoyed it.

Lewis:

If I didn't enjoy writing I wouldn't continue to do it. Of all my books, there was only one I did not take pleasure in writing.

Mr Wirt:

Which one?

Lewis:

The Screwtape Letters. They were dry and gritty going. At the time, I was thinking of objections to the Christian life, and decided to put them into the form, "That's what the Devil would say." But making goods "bad" and bads "good" gets to be fatiguing.

Mr Wirt:

How would you suggest a young Christian writer go about developing a style?

Lewis:

The way for a person to develop a style is (a) to know

[8] Except for slight variations in the wording, Aslan says this to two children who ask him about other people's lives in *The Horse and His Boy* (London, 1954), ch. xi, p. 147 and ch. xiv, p. 180.

[9] I Corinthians iii. 6.

[10] "Usually the way must be made ready for heaven, and then it will come by some other; the sacrifice must be made ready, and the fire will strike on another altar." Charles Williams, *He Came Down from Heaven* (London, 1938), ch. ii, p. 25.

exactly what he wants to say, and (b) to be sure he is saying exactly that. The reader, we must remember, does not start by knowing what we mean. If our words are ambiguous, our meaning will escape him. I sometimes think that writing is like driving sheep down a road. If there is any gate open to the left or the right the readers will most certainly go into it.

Mr Wirt:

Do you believe that the Holy Spirit can speak to the world through Christian writers today?

Lewis:

I prefer to make no judgment concerning a writer's direct "illumination" by the Holy Spirit. I have no way of knowing whether what is written is from heaven or not. I do believe that God is the Father of lights—natural lights as well as spiritual lights (James i. 17). That is, God is not interested only in Christian writers as such. He is concerned with all kinds of writing. In the same way a sacred calling is not limited to ecclesiastical functions. The man who is weeding a field of turnips is also serving God.

Mr Wirt:

An American writer, Mr. Dewey Beegle, has stated that in his opinion the Isaac Watts hymn, "When I Survey the Wondrous Cross," is more inspired by God than is the "Song of Solomon" in the Old Testament. What would be your view?

Lewis:

The great saints and mystics of the church have felt just the opposite about it. They have found tremendous spiritual truth in the "Song of Solomon." There is a difference of levels here. The question of the canon is involved. Also we must remember that what is meat for a grown person might be unsuited to the palate of a child.

Mr Wirt:

How would you evaluate modern literary trends as exemplified by such writers as Ernest Hemingway, Samuel Beckett, and Jean-Paul Sartre?

Lewis:

I have read very little in the field. I am not a contemporary

scholar. I am not even a scholar of the past, but I am a lover
of the past.

Mr Wirt:

Do you believe that the use of filth and obscenity is necessary in order to establish a realistic atmosphere in contemporary literature?

Lewis:

I do not. I treat this development as a symptom, a sign of
a culture that has lost its faith. Moral collapse follows upon
spiritual collapse. I look upon the immediate future with great
apprehension.

Mr Wirt:

Do you feel, then, that modern culture is being de-Chris-
tianized?

Lewis:

I cannot speak to the political aspects of the question, but
I have some definite views about the de-Christianizing of the
church. I believe that there are many accommodating preachers,
and too many practitioners in the church who are not believers.
Jesus Christ did not say, "Go into all the world and tell the
world that it is quite right." The Gospel is something completely
different. In fact, it is directly opposed to the world.

The case against Christianity that is made out in the world
is quite strong. Every war, every shipwreck, every cancer case,
every calamity, contributes to making a *prima facie* case against
Christianity. It is not easy to be a believer in the face of this
surface evidence. It calls for a strong faith in Jesus Christ.

Mr Wirt:

Do you approve of men such as Bryan Green and Billy
Graham asking people to come to a point of decision regarding
the Christian life?

Lewis:

I had the pleasure of meeting Billy Graham once. We had
dinner together during his visit to Cambridge University in
1955, while he was conducting a mission to students. I thought
he was a very modest and a very sensible man, and I liked him
very much indeed.

In a civilization like ours, I feel that everyone has to come to terms with the claims of Jesus Christ upon his life, or else be guilty of inattention or of evading the question. In the Soviet Union it is different. Many people living in Russia today have never had to consider the claims of Christ because they have never heard of those claims.

In the same way, we who live in English-speaking countries have never really been forced to consider the claims, let us say, of Hinduism. But in our Western civilization we are obligated both morally and intellectually to come to grips with Jesus Christ; if we refuse to do so we are guilty of being bad philosophers and bad thinkers.

Mr Wirt:

What is your view of the daily discipline of the Christian life—the need for taking time to be alone with God?

Lewis:

We have our New Testament regimental orders upon the subject. I would take it for granted that everyone who becomes a Christian would undertake this practice. It is enjoined upon us by our Lord; and since they are His commands, I believe in following them. It is always just possible that Jesus Christ meant what He said when He told us to seek the secret place and to close the door.[11]

Mr Wirt:

What do you think is going to happen in the next few years of history, Mr. Lewis?

Lewis:

I have no way of knowing. My primary field is the past. I travel with my back to the engine, and that makes it difficult when you try to steer. The world might stop in ten minutes; meanwhile, we are to go on doing our duty. The great thing is to be found at one's post as a child of God, living each day as though it were our last, but planning as though our world might last a hundred years.

We have, of course, the assurance of the New Testament regarding events to come.[12] I find it difficult to keep from

[11]Matthew vi. 5–6.
[12]Matthew xxiv. 4–44; Mark xiii. 5–27; Luke xxi. 8–33.

laughing when I find people worrying about future destruction of some kind or other. Didn't they know they were going to die anyway? Apparently not. My wife once asked a young woman friend whether she had ever thought of death, and she replied, "By the time I reach that age science will have done something about it!"

Mr Wirt:

Do you think there will be widespread travel in space?

Lewis:

I look forward with horror to contact with the other inhabited planets, if there are such. We would only transport to them all of our sin and our acquisitiveness, and establish a new colonialism. I can't bear to think of it. But if we on earth were to get right with God, of course, all would be changed. Once we find ourselves spiritually awakened, we can go to outer space and take the good things with us. That is quite a different matter.

25.

THE SERMON
AND THE LUNCH

AND SO," SAID THE PREACHER "THE HOME MUST BE THE FOUN-dation of our national life. It is there, all said and done, that character is formed. It is there that we appear as we really are. It is there we can fling aside the weary disguises of the outer world and be ourselves. It is there that we retreat from the noise and stress and temptation and dissipation of daily life to seek the sources of fresh strength and renewed purity. . . ." And as he spoke I noticed that all confidence in him had departed from every member of that congregation who was under thirty. They had been listening well up to this point. Now the shuf-flings and coughings began. Pews creaked; muscles relaxed. The sermon, for all practical purposes, was over; the five min-utes for which the preacher continued talking were a total waste of time—at least for most of us.

Whether I wasted them or not is for you to judge. I certainly did not hear any more of the sermon. I was thinking; and the starting point of my thought was the question, "How can he? How can *he* of all people?" For I knew the preacher's own home pretty well. In fact, I had been lunching there that very day, making a fifth to the vicar and the vicar's wife and the son (R.A.F.)[1] and the daughter (A.T.S.),[2] who happened both to be on leave. I could have avoided it, but the girl had whis-pered to me, "For God's sake stay to lunch if they ask you. It's always a little less frightful when there's a visitor."

Lunch at the vicarage nearly always follows the same pat-tern. It starts with a desperate attempt on the part of the young people to keep up a bright patter of trivial conversation: trivial not because they are trivially minded (you can have real con-versation with them if you get them alone), but because it would

[1]Royal Air Force.
[2]Auxiliary Territorial Service.

161

never occur to either of them to say at home anything they were really thinking, unless it is forced out of them by anger. They are talking only to try to keep their parents quiet. They fail. The vicar, ruthlessly interrupting, cuts in on a quite different subject. He is telling us how to reeducate Germany. He has never been there and seems to know nothing either of German history or the German language. "But, father," begins the son, and gets no further. His mother is now talking, though nobody knows exactly when she began. She is in the middle of a complicated story about how badly some neighbor has treated her. Though it goes on a long time, we never learn either how it began or how it ended: it is all middle. "Mother, that's not quite fair," says the daughter at last. "Mrs. Walker never said—" but her father's voice booms in again. He is telling his son about the organization of the R.A.F. So it goes on until either the vicar or his wife says something so preposterous that the boy or the girl contradicts and insists on making the contradiction heard. The real minds of the young people have at last been called into action. They talk fiercely, quickly, contemptuously. They have facts and logic on their side. There is an answering flare-up from the parents. The father storms; the mother is (oh, blessed domestic queen's move!) "hurt"— plays pathos for all she is worth. The daughter becomes ironical. The father and son, elaborately ignoring each other, start talking to me. The lunch party is in ruins.

The memory of that lunch worries me during the last few minutes of the sermon. I am not worried by the fact that the vicar's practice differs from his precept. That is, no doubt, regrettable, but it is nothing to the purpose. As Dr. Johnson said, precept may be very sincere (and, let us add, very profitable) where practice is very imperfect,[3] and no one but a fool would discount a doctor's warnings about alcoholic poisoning because the doctor himself drank too much. What worries me is the fact that the vicar is not telling us at all that home life is difficult and has, like every form of life, its own proper temptations and corruptions. He keeps on talking as if "home" were a panacea, a magical charm which of itself was bound to produce happiness and virtue. The trouble is not that he is insincere but that he is a fool. He is not talking from his own experience of family life at all: he is automatically reproducing

[3]James Boswell, *Life of Johnson*, ed. George Birkbeck Hill (Oxford, 1934), vol. IV, p. 397 (December 2, 1784).

a sentimental tradition—and it happens to be a false tradition. That is why the congregation have stopped listening to him.

If Christian teachers wish to recall Christian people to domesticity—and I, for one, believe that people must be recalled to it—the first necessity is to stop telling lies about home life and to substitute realistic teaching. Perhaps the fundamental principles would be something like this.

1. Since the Fall no organization or way of life whatever has a natural tendency to go right. In the Middle Ages some people thought that if only they entered a religious order they would find themselves automatically becoming holy and happy: the whole native literature of the period echoes with the exposure of that fatal error. In the nineteenth century some people thought that monogamous family life would automatically make them holy and happy; the savage antidomestic literature of modern times—the Samuel Butlers, the Gosses, the Shaws— delivered the answer. In both cases the "debunkers" may have been wrong about principles and may have forgotten the maxim *abusus non tollit usum*:[4] but in both cases they were pretty right about matter of fact. Both family life and monastic life were often detestable, and it should be noticed that the serious defenders of both are well aware of the dangers and free of the sentimental illusion. The author of the *Imitation of Christ* knows (no one better) how easily monastic life goes wrong. Charlotte M. Yonge makes it abundantly clear that domesticity is no passport to heaven on earth but an arduous vocation—a sea full of hidden rocks and perilous ice shores only to be navigated by one who uses a celestial chart. That is the first point on which we must be absolutely clear. The family, like the nation, can be offered to God, can be converted and redeemed, and will then become the channel of particular blessings and graces. But, like everything else that is human, it needs redemption. Unredeemed, it will produce only particular temptations, corruptions, and miseries. Charity begins at home: so does uncharity.

2. By the conversion or sanctification of family life we must be careful to mean something more than the preservation of "love" in the sense of natural affection. Love (in that sense) is not enough. Affection, as distinct from charity, is not a cause of lasting happiness. Left to its natural bent affection becomes in the end greedy, naggingly solicitous, jealous, exacting, ti-

---

[4] "The abuse does not abolish the use."

morous. It suffers agony when its object is absent—but is not
repaid by any long enjoyment when the object is present. Even
at the vicar's lunch table affection was partly the cause of the
quarrel. That son would have borne patiently and humorously
from any other old man the silliness which enraged him in his
father. It is because he still (in some fashion) "cares" that he
is impatient. The vicar's wife would not be quite that endless
whimper of self-pity which she now is if she did not (in a sense)
"love" the family: the continued disappointment of her continued and ruthless demand for sympathy, for affection, for ap-
preciation has helped to make her what she is. I do not think
this aspect of affection is nearly enough noticed by most popular
moralists. The greed to be loved is a fearful thing. Some of
those who say (and almost with pride) that they live only for
love come, at last, to live in incessant resentment.

3. We must realize the yawning pitfall in that very characteristic of home life which is so often glibly paraded as its
principal attraction. "It is there that we appear as we really are:
it is there that we can fling aside the disguises and be ourselves."
These words, in the vicar's mouth, were only too true and he
showed at the lunch table what they meant. Outside his own
house he behaves with ordinary courtesy. He would not have
interrupted any other young man as he interrupted his son. He
would not, in any other society, have talked confident nonsense
about subjects of which he was totally ignorant: or, if he had,
he would have accepted correction with good temper. In fact,
he values home as the place where he can "be himself" in the
sense of trampling on all the restraints which civilized humanity
has found indispensable for tolerable social intercourse. And
this, I think, is very common. What chiefly distinguishes domestic from public conversation is surely very often simply its
downright rudeness. What distinguishes domestic behavior is
often its selfishness, slovenliness, incivility—even brutality.
And it will often happen that those who praise home life most
loudly are the worst offenders in this respect: they praise it—
they are always glad to get home, hate the outer world, can't
stand visitors, can't be bothered meeting people, etc.—because
the freedoms in which they indulge themselves at home have
ended by making them unfit for civilized society. If they practiced elsewhere the only behavior they now find "natural" they
would simply be knocked down.

4. How, then, *are* people to behave at home? If a man can't
be comfortable and unguarded, can't take his ease and "be

himself" in his own house, where can he? That is, I confess, the trouble. The answer is an alarming one. There is *nowhere* this side of heaven where one can safely lay the reins on the horse's neck. It will never be lawful simply to "be ourselves" until "ourselves" have become sons of God. It is all there in the hymn—"Christian, seek not yet repose." This does not mean, of course, that there is no difference between home life and general society. It does mean that home life has its own rule of courtesy—a code more intimate, more subtle, more sensitive, and, therefore, in some ways more difficult, than that of the outer world.

5. Finally, must we not teach that if the home is to be a means of grace it must be a place of *rules?* There cannot be a common life without a *regula*. The alternative to rule is not freedom but the unconstitutional (and often unconscious) tyranny of the most selfish member.

In a word, must we not either cease to preach domesticity or else begin to preach it seriously? Must we not abandon sentimental eulogies and begin to give practical advice on the high, hard, lovely, and adventurous art of really creating the Christian family?

26.

WHAT CHRISTMAS MEANS TO ME

THREE THINGS GO BY THE NAME OF CHRISTMAS. ONE IS A
religious festival. This is important and obligatory for Christians; but as it can be of no interest to anyone else, I shall
naturally say no more about it here. The second (it has complex
historical connections with the first, but we needn't go into
them) is a popular holiday, an occasion for merrymaking and
hospitality. If it were my business to have a "view" on this, I
should say that I much approve of merrymaking. But what I
approve of much more is everybody minding his own business.
I see no reason why I should volunteer views as to how other
people should spend their own money in their own leisure
among their own friends. It is highly probable that they want
my advice on such matters as little as I want theirs. But the
third thing called Christmas is unfortunately everyone's business.

I mean of course the commercial racket. The interchange
of presents was a very small ingredient in the older English
festivity. Mr. Pickwick took a cod with him to Dingley Dell;
the reformed Scrooge ordered a turkey for his clerk; lovers sent
love gifts; toys and fruit were given to children. But the idea
that not only all friends but even all acquaintances should give
one another presents, or at least send one another cards, is quite
modern and has been forced upon us by the shopkeepers. Neither of these circumstances is in itself a reason for condemning
it. I condemn it on the following grounds.

1. It gives on the whole much more pain than pleasure. You
have only to stay over Christmas with a family who seriously
try to "keep" it (in its third, or commercial, aspect) in order
to see that the thing is a nightmare. Long before December 25,
everyone is worn out—physically worn out by weeks of daily
struggle in overcrowded shops, mentally worn out by the effort
to remember all the right recipients and to think out suitable

gifts for them. They are in no trim for merrymaking; much less (if they should want to) to take part in a religious act. They look far more as if there had been a long illness in the house.

2. Most of it is involuntary. The modern rule is that anyone can force you to give him a present by sending you a quite unprovoked present of his own. It is almost a blackmail. Who has not heard the wail of despair, and indeed of resentment, when, at the last moment, just as everyone hoped that the nuisance was over for one more year, the unwanted gift from Mrs. Busy (whom we hardly remember) flops unwelcomed through the letter box, and back to the dreadful shops one of us has to go?

3. Things are given as presents which no mortal ever bought for himself—gaudy and useless gadgets, "novelties" because no one was ever fool enough to make their like before. Have we really no better use for materials and for human skill and time than to spend them on all this rubbish?

4. The nuisance. For after all, during the racket we still have all our ordinary and necessary shopping to do, and the racket trebles the labor of it.

We are told that the whole dreary business must go on because it is good for trade. It is in fact merely one annual symptom of that lunatic condition of our country, and indeed of the world, in which everyone lives by persuading everyone else to buy things. I don't know the way out. But can it really be my duty to buy and receive masses of junk every winter just to help the shopkeepers? If the worst comes to the worst I'd sooner give them money for nothing and write it off as a charity. For nothing? Why, better for nothing than for a nuisance.

Also available...the complete edition of
GOD IN THE DOCK
Essays on Theology and Ethics
by C. S. Lewis
Edited by Walter Hooper

Published by Wm. B. Eerdmans Publishing Co.
255 Jefferson Ave., S.E.
Grand Rapids, Michigan 49503

From *The New York Times* Book Review...
"The searching mind and the poetic spirit of C. S. Lewis
are readily evident in this collection of essays edited by his
one-time secretary, Walter Hooper. Here the reader finds
the tough-minded polemicist relishing the debate; here too
the kindly teacher explaining a complex abstraction by means
of clarifying analogies; here the public speaker addressing
his varied audience with all the humility and grace of a man
who knows how much more remains to be unknown."

ABOUT THE AUTHOR

C. S. LEWIS, a contemporary and friend of J. R. R. Tolkien, has emerged as the twentieth century's greatest apologist for the Christian faith. Since his death on the day of John F. Kennedy's assassination, November 22, 1963, his popularity has been constantly on the rise. He is best known for his children's fantasy series *The Chronicles of Narnia*, his science-fiction trilogy *Out of the Silent Planet, Perelandra, That Hideous Strength*, his theology work *Mere Christianity*, and his delightful allegory *Screwtape Letters*. *The Grand Miracle* is a collection of some of his finest essays, which should be a welcome addition to anyone's shelf of C. S. Lewis literature.

EPIPHANY

MORE INSPIRATIONAL PAPERBACKS
FROM BALLANTINE BOOKS 🆒